D1538254

OPEN HEAVENS

DAVID GRECO

THOMAS NELSON PUBLISHERS
Nashville

Scripture quotations are from the New King James Version of the Bible © 1982 by Thomas Nelson Publishers.

Open Heavens was translated *Cielos Abiertos* (Spanish) by Oscar Sadder.

Library of Congress Cataloging-in-Publication Data

Greco, David.
  [Cielos abiertos. English]
   Open heavens: unlock the power of revival in your life / David Greco.
     p. cm.
   ISBN 0-7852-4606-1
    1. Spiritual life—Christianity. I. Title.
BV4506.G7413 2001
243—dc21   00–053710

Printed in the United States of America
1 2 3 4 5 6 7 — 06 05 04 03 02 01

Dedication

This book is dedicated to my brother, my friend, and God's servant, Rhadames Fernandez, pastor of Amanacer de la Esperanza *(Dawn of Hope), Bronx, New York.*

Acknowledgments

To my beloved wife, Denise, my prayer warrior

To the staff members at *Radio Vision Cristiana* (Radio Christian Vision) with whom I first began to see open heavens

To the army of God in the New York metropolitan area

To the tribe of Judah (you know who you are)

To the Christian people of Cuba

Table of Contents

Introduction

"What would Jesus do?" is the greatest question asked in the 1900s. It has survived its infancy in Charles Sheldon's little turn-of-the-century novel, and gone on to achieve fame and longevity on the wristbands, Bible covers, and dashboard décor of the millennial generation.

What, then, is the question for our moment? Perhaps: How did Jesus do it?

These are powerful days for the church of the Lord Jesus Christ around the world. It's a time of excitement and renewed passion for God. Miraculous healings, restorations, and salvations are on the rise, as is the air of expectancy among believers. Those we thought would resist Jesus to their graves are embracing and bowing down to Him. Jewish people are turning to Him of their own free will as never before in history and are forming multiple congregations in the Americas, Eastern Europe and in Israel itself. Fortresses of Islam have been breached and are being brought down worldwide, though Muslims who turn to Jesus know that literal death at the hands of their neighbors may follow.

In this atmosphere of miracles, believers have an unfulfilled desire: I want to, I need to, be more like Jesus. Just like the early disciples, we see the miracles, we are even active participants at times. But then we are left to confront the fact that whatever Jesus had apparently hasn't transferred to us. It's been a challenge for the church since it began. We can love Jesus. After all, He's done so much for us. And, as evidenced by the signs and wonders all around us in our day, He is still active today. But we can't really be like Him, can we? After all, we are human; He is God.

Yet, before He left the earth, He told us we would do greater works even than those He had done. Most of us have not grappled with, let alone achieved the outworking of this promise. This promise is different than His admonition to us to do as He commands us. That one is easier to grasp and, admittedly, to preach.

Do we want to be like Jesus? Do we want to do what He did? What do the few throughout history who seem to have walked as Jesus walked know that the rest of us don't? What do they do that we don't?

✸ The secret is living a life under open heavens. This means living in daily, unhindered two-way communication with God the Father. It means walking with a God-revealed understanding of His original plans and purposes for the universe. What God wanted for His creation was not a world of rules and rituals and good habits and nice manners, or even of deep thinking and great teaching. He wanted relationship. And His design would be that, as relating back and forth would please Him, it would also satisfy us. Everything He has done with the earth and its people since then has been aimed at restoring that perfect fellowship known only in heaven and in Eden.

His dealings throughout history-with Israel and with the church right up through today-all point toward this aim, if only we would see it. And perhaps we can see it if we look again with fresh eyes at the life of Jesus. The church stands at the brink of the fulfillment of many long-awaited promises. We may very soon see the plans and purposes of God expounded not only from pulpits but from people's lives as we grapple with our destiny as God's people, God's army, the keepers of His presence in this world.

What would Jesus do? We think we know, but as a body we haven't seen it travel from the head to the hands and feet.

How, then, did Jesus do it? He lived under open heavens and pointed the way for us-His people, His brothers, His body, His army, His bride—to do the same.

For the earth will be filled with the knowledge of the glory of the Lord, as the waters cover the sea.

Habbakuk 2:14

May we see the promise fulfilled in our day.

■ David Greco

1

The All in All: God's Original Intent

Have you ever thought that if you could just reach a certain spiritual level, you would have reached the top? I used to think that way. But after a few years of being molded by God, I realized that there are no pinnacles in God—there is no "maximum level." We are never finished.

God's core purpose is to become the center.

God made us, loves us and has crafted an inheritance for us that includes an array of promises. But His ultimate plan is not limited to the fulfillment of these promises—the Christian "wish list." There is an ultimate fulfillment toward which He has been working since creation, toward which all His dealings with the people of earth have been aimed, and toward which the Church of the Lord Jesus Christ is being propelled in these days as never before.

God's core purpose is to become the center. "The center of what?" you may ask. The center of everything: human activity, the natural world, the movements of the stars and planets, the movements of angels and demons, every man and every woman, every law, every value, every meaning, every event and ultimately the center of your heart.

He would be the all in all.

But He is God, you say. Is He not the all in all? He merits this place, certainly. But He Himself has said in His word that He does not have it as He wants. It is toward this restoration that all His dealings with man have been aimed. And it was for this primary purpose that Jesus came and is now at work with His church.

> *"Then comes the end, when He (Christ) delivers the kingdom to God the Father, when He puts an end to all rule and all authority and power. For He must reign till He has put all enemies under His feet. The last enemy that will be destroyed is death . . . Now when all things are made subject to Him, then the Son Himself will also be subject to Him who put all things under Him, that God may be all in all."*
>
> I Corinthians 15:24–26,28; emphasis added

Every Christian has an individual encounter with Jesus the Savior. At the moment of salvation, a person accepts that only Jesus can redeem him from death and give eternal life. God then takes the person "out of Egypt," frees him from the claws of the devil and the bondage of sin, and introduces him to his inheritance of promises—the last and best of which is life in heaven forever with Him.

But the basic truth is this: we are not saved only to go to heaven. We are saved so that God may establish His rule in every area of our lives and, as a result, we may serve as an example to those who do not believe.

That is God's intent. He wants us to live out His government, His laws, before the world. And while this can be done at one level in the life of the individual believer, it is most fully accomplished when the people of God live it out as a body.

---

*The missing element has been
open heavens.*

You can see the hand of God propelling His people toward this end in His dealings with Israel. You can also see it—if you take a fresh look at all you have been taught—in Jesus' work on earth, the work He is still doing from His place at the right hand of the Father. And you can see it in the movement of the Holy Spirit in the church worldwide today.

Why is God still not the all in all in the universe? Why, even, is He still not at the center of the lives of His people? Why is His kingdom not established over His people? Over individuals, yes. Even the world can point to a few individuals who model complete surrender to living under God's rule. But as a model of life under the government of God, His body has far to go.

The missing element has been open heavens.

I've had the opportunity to preach all over the United States and Latin America in the last few years. When I preach to Latin audiences in the states—in Miami, New York City, California, the Southwest—I battle a certain resistance. But when I've taken the same message to areas in Latin America, people run to the altars by the thousands in response. Same message, same messenger, presented in essentially the same culture. Different response. Why? Open heavens over the region.

At its most basic level, open heavens is direct, two-way communication between God and His people, unimpeded by sin, Satan or the world. We have 2000 years of church history to show that we are not yet formed as a body living fully under the government of God, moving in response to His voice, He responding to ours. But we also have some evidence from around the world that God's original intent is beginning to be realized.

═══════════◆═══════════

Israel's inheritance was the reign of God in all situations.

I will try to paint the picture of life under open heavens in the coming chapters using brushstrokes from God's dealings with Israel, His still unfolding work through His Son and the evidence of His movements through the Holy Spirit today. We will see that over and over again, God's pattern and plan has been to use a people, not a collection of sanctified persons. This is His ultimate destination. And while God may place conditions on His promises to us at times, making them dependent on our response, He always fulfills His purposes, always reaches His ultimate goals.

The Two Frontiers

Israel had two frontiers. One was Egypt. It represented a life of oppression under an exploitive government. The other was Canaan, the land flowing with milk and honey. For 40 years, the Israelites lived between frontiers. They would not go back to Egypt. Neither would they enter the promised land. What was God's purpose in taking them out of Egypt? Just to bring them to Canaan? The Bible tells us:

> *"You will bring them in and plant them in the mountain of your inheritance, in the place, O Lord, which you have made for Your own dwelling, the sanctuary, O Lord, which your hands have established. The Lord shall reign forever and ever."*
>
> Exodus 15:17–18

God's purpose for Israel was:

- To bring them to the promised land
- Plant them firmly in their inheritance
- Establish a sanctuary of His glory and share it with His people
- Establish His kingdom and rule in Israel as an example to all nations

God's will was not only to give the people the land they would inhabit. The Lord took the Israelites to the Promised Land with one chief purpose: to reign over them, directly and without intervention. But for 40 years, Israel vacillated between frontiers because they did not understand God's purpose. (They did not understand that their inheritance was the presence of God among them.) What a privilege they had! No other people before or since could claim the inheritance of a continuous, glorious presence of God. No other people could claim that their king was the God who created the heavens and the earth, and who was perfect in all His ways.

Israel's inheritance was the reign of God in all situations. The people needed to understand that the inheritance was not the land. Their inheritance was God, the king of Israel, the Sovereign One who, in the midst of every desert in which His people find themselves, rises up to show His power.

The Spirit of Egypt

The enemy that held Israel then and has held back the church today may be identified as the spirit of Egypt.

We are so easily enticed to worship idols, even calling them God, or Christianizing them.

Israel had been in slavery for over 400 years. During that time they absorbed the "spirit of Egypt:"

1. Their concept of economy was based on the fact that the Nile River was the main source of water, irrigation for their crops and source of food. The Nile was deep and generous. It came from the high snow-capped mountains in the heart of Africa. Egypt looked to the Nile as their source of life, food and economy. They trusted the Nile.

2. The pharaoh was the ruler of Egypt. He was the visible symbol of power and authority. He was their leader in prosperity and in times of war. He was their ruler and their general. However, this leadership was that of a harsh slave master. A wounded Israel began to connect "authority" with abuse.

3.   Egypt worshiped visible gods—images of rock, wood, and precious metals.

Now, God's purpose with Israel was different. In order for God to be the all in all to Israel, the spirit of Egypt had to be eradicated from the mind of Israel. Look what God had in mind for them in the Promised Land:

1.   Their economy, food and source of water was not based on a river. The Jordan was not large enough to maintain the whole nation. So, God said to them that if they would obey His commandments and live under His rule, He would send rain from heaven. In the Promised land, their source of life would be God, not a river as in Egypt.
2.   God, not a human ruler, was to be king. God would give them priests as go-betweens or spokesmen, but He would be the ultimate authority. The authority in Israel would not be a visible leader, but God, an invisible King. God was not a slave master like Pharaoh. He was a caring Father who wanted to lead them as His children.
3.   God prohibited the worship of images. He was spirit, unlike the Egyptian gods.

It is very easy to see why there are not open heavens over our lives, over our cities. God is not our source. God is not our ruler. God is not our only object of worship. We base our prosperity on our talents, economy, money and ideas. We would rather be ruled by human laws, human committees and regulations than by the Spirit of God. And we are so easily enticed to worship idols, even calling them God, or Christianizing them. We still have a slave mentality. On the one hand, we obey only out of obligation or fear of reprisal. On the other, we become preoccupied with developing rules and regulations to prevent abuse of authority.

Miracles in the Midst of the Desert

God began showing Himself in miraculous ways the moment He brought the people out of Egypt. He separated the waters of the Red Sea, destroyed the Egyptian army and took the Israelites to Mount Sinai, that they might see with their natural eyes the manifestation of the presence of God. Camped out in the valley below, they could do nothing for 40 days but stand in awe as the earth trembled, and lightning and fire came down from the mountain. God promised to be everything to them. He allowed them to hear the roar of His voice, and to see the glory of His presence manifested visibly on Moses' face. There was no doubt that He was with Israel, that He was their king, and that He was more powerful than Pharaoh and the gods of Egypt.

After restoring the bitter waters of Marah, God told them:

> *"If you listen carefully to the voice of the Lord your God and do what is right in His eyes, if you pay attention to His commands, and keep all His decrees, I will not bring on you any of the diseases I brought on the Egyptians, for I am the Lord who heals you."*
>
> Exodus 15:26 NIV

God drew water from the rock for the Israelites to drink. He gave them bread from heaven every day, as the skies rained manna. When they wanted meat, He sent them quail. Jehovah always went before them; His presence surrounded them day and night. The Lord was their everything, their all in all. This is how the Bible tells it:

> *"The Lord went before them by day in a pillar of cloud to lead the way, and by night in a pillar of fire to give them light, so as to go by day and night. He did not take away the pillar of cloud by day or the pillar of fire by night from before the people."*
>
> Exodus 13:21–22

God provided. They had enough. God was in the process of eradicating the spirit of Egypt. Even though there was no river, God gave them water. Even though they had no food, God gave them manna in the desert. God was teaching them the principle of His Kingdom.

◆

In our lives, idols will arise that seem to offer us help in the desert.

But the same old serpent that tempted Eve tempted the Israelites in the desert. Between Egypt and the Promised Land, complaints and discontent arose among them and they erected an idol—a golden calf. The spirit of Egypt rose up. They needed a visible god like the Egyptians.

Temptations in the Desert

When God wants to establish himself as king of our lives, a challenge always presents itself. In Israel's case, a golden calf made by their own hands was the challenge. In Christians, it begins at the moment we meet the Savior. God brings forth His eternal purpose. He brings us toward the fulfillment of promise in our lives. I assure you that at some point in this process an idol will arise to try to question the total Lordship of God in your life.

An idol is something that resembles the genuine, something or someone that tries to replace the authentic and the real. In our lives, idols will arise that seem to offer us help in the desert. They may take the form of family, career, position, influence, the environment etc. Any one of these things may entice us to put it in the place God should occupy as the all in all, the source of everything.

When the Israelites realized that Moses was not coming down from the mountain, they told Aaron, "Come, make us gods that shall go before us." (Exodus 32:1) The word "go" as used here, in Hebrew means "to walk facing forward, as a leader." With this dramatic petition, the Israelites were asking for the presence of another god as a guide. They remembered that Egypt was powerful because they were led by visible gods. This invisible god concept was ridiculous!

God will never be thwarted
in His purposes.

"All the people broke off the golden earrings which were in their ears and brought them to Aaron. And he received the gold from their hand, and he fashioned it with an engraving tool, and made a molded calf.

"Then they said, 'This is your god, O Israel, that

brought you out of the land of Egypt.' So, when Aaron saw it, he built an altar before it. And Aaron made a proclamation and said, "Tomorrow is a feast to the Lord." He called the calf "Lord" or "Jehovah." Israel did not want to totally reject their God Jehovah, they wanted an idol in a visible form that would make them feel secure in the wilderness. They wanted a visible Jehovah!

The people had forgotten everything. God, the Great I Am, was not enough. They chose to defy the Kingship of God that demanded obedience and faithfulness.

When they were about to reach the Promised Land, in the land of the Edomites, the Israelites again decided to defy God. They became discouraged and began to murmur:

> *"The people spoke against God and against Moses: 'Why have you brought us up out of Egypt to die in the wilderness? For there is no food and no water and our soul loathes this worthless bread.'"*

Numbers 21:5

Although God supplied water from the rock and manna from heaven, the Israelites loathed or detested it. They felt disgust at what God was supplying for them. The spirit of Egypt caused them to want food and water on demand. They did not want to wait for the providence of God. They were used to a river-based economy.

That's why He sent the snakes that killed many in the camp. Since Israel forgot and defied His kingship, God sent one of the plagues He had sent to Egypt: death. That is what Egypt eventually produces: death.

God will never be thwarted in His purposes. At

times, His promises are conditional, dependent on our response. But His purposes are immovable.

The people of Israel were the first example of God's government to the nations. God gave Moses the Law. In the Law, He wanted to show the world that under His government, man could have communion with Him by means of sacrifice. He wanted His people to be obedient and develop holy character. If they did, God provided protection, food, health and peace.

The form of God's dealings with man have changed. The requirement of sacrifice as the means to communion with Him passed away with the beautiful provision of Jesus. But His original intent has not changed. His purpose is still to be "the all in all." (I Cor. 15:28) The word *purpose* in Greek is *prothesis. Pro* means "before or previous" and *thesis* means "intention." Therefore, purpose is an original intention, or a previous position. God has always decreed that He would be the all in all. That has never changed.

But the fulfillment of His purpose has yet to be realized. The thwarting of that purpose began long ago.

The Fall of the Angel

There was a time when God was truly the center of the universe. All of creation operated in perfect order, as He had designed it to do. "The morning stars sang together and all the sons of God shouted for joy. (Job 38:7) This scene included the angels, whom the Bible says were as the stars or as the sons of God. They worshiped God alone with absolute holiness and purity. He was the all in all in each angel and creation brought forth perfect and holy worship. Don't imagine that God is an egotist.

He did not need the worship of His creation. But creation operates in harmony when God is the center of its purpose and worship.

God was the absolute center of all praise and admiration. The universe operated perfectly in harmony and beauty. God had placed each celestial body in its place, with the purpose of rendering unto Him perfect glory and praise: "The heavens declare the glory of God." (Psalm 19:1)

◆

A scheme took root in his heart and he tried to invade the place that belonged only to God.

But the time came when Lucifer defied the absolute Lordship of God over all:

"I will ascend into heaven, I will exalt my throne above the stars of God; I will also sit on the mount of the congregation on the farthest sides of the north; I will ascend above the heights of the clouds, I will be like the Most High."

Isaiah 14:13–14

Lucifer, the son of the morning (a star of the dawn), worshiped God. God was the center of his worship and his existence. Lucifer existed with the sole purpose of worshipping and exalting God. But at some point, he became dissatisfied with his own place of perfection, a scheme took root in his heart and he tried to invade the place that belonged only to God. At that moment, God ceased to be the all in all for Lucifer, and so came his fall; "How are you fallen from heaven, O Lucifer, son of

the morning! How are you cut down to the ground!"
(Isaiah 14:12)

The prophet Ezekiel tells it this way: "Son of man,
take up a lamentation for the king of Tyre, and say to
him, 'Thus says the Lord God:

> *"You were the seal of perfection, Full of wisdom and perfect
> in beauty. You were in Eden, the garden of God; every pre-
> cious stone was your covering: the sardius, topaz and dia-
> mond, beryl, onyx, and jasper, sapphire, turquoise, and
> emerald with gold. The workmanship of your timbrels and
> pipes was prepared for you on the day you were created.*
>
> *You were the anointed cherub who covers; I established
> you; You were on the only mountain of God; You walked back
> and forth in the midst of fiery stones. You were perfect in
> your ways from the day you were created, until iniquity was
> found in you.*
>
> *By the abundance of your trading you became filled with
> violence within, and you sinned; therefore I cast you as a
> profane thing out of the mountain of God; And I destroyed
> you, O covering cherub, from the midst of the fiery stones.*
>
> *Your heart was lifted up because of your beauty; you
> corrupted your wisdom for the sake of your splendor; I cast
> you to the ground, I laid you before kings, that they might
> gaze at you."*

Ezekiel 28:12–17

There is no doubt that at some point, God was
everything in everyone. He was the center of the universe. Everyone worshiped Him with absolute faithfulness. His Lordship was not defied and was accepted
without reserve. All of creation was absolutely submitted
to the justice of God.

The Inheritance of Rebellion

God ceased to be the all in all when Lucifer, the covering cherub, defied Him. At that same moment, the curse entered creation. Ever since, the covering or protective cherub is the one who defies God and tries to corrupt all creation. That blemished being tries to mark others. The curse of disobedience and rebellion against the absolute kingship of God is manifested in Lucifer. Therefore, God throws him to earth.

In His absolute mercy and love, God prepared creation and set Adam as the center, He made Him a little lower than the angels. He crowned him with glory and honor and set him before all creation (Read Hebrews 2:7–8). God put him in the Garden of Eden and gave him free will: the power to choose who would be his Lord.

God was the everything in Adam. God was the everything in Eve. But the perfect balance was already ruined. Lucifer came to Eve as a serpent and tempted her with the idea that God was not the all in all, that man could be like God and could share the lordship of everything. Man was created to submit to the government of God. But in his rebellion, he took a place that did not belong to him, a place of choosing between good and evil.

God ceased to be the all in all in Adam and Eve when they disobeyed the clear orders of their creator. Creation was thus thrown off balance. The curse of Lucifer corrupted Adam and Eve and all their descendants. As a consequence, Cain killed his brother and descendants were violent. Humanity suffered violence because God was not the center of all. Man began to depend on his own knowledge and judgment of what was right and good.

Today, we can see what happens in our society when man places himself at the center of creation and forgets about God. Man takes it upon himself to decide what is evil or good, what he should accept or reject, with disastrous results.

So, then, is there hope? Yes, God gives us a promise.

Restoration

God made a promise of salvation and restoration. It decrees that His position as the all in all will be restored by somebody that will come from the seed of the woman:

> *"And I will put enmity between you and the woman and between your seed and her Seed; He shall bruise your head and you shall bruise his heel."*

Genesis 3:15

The seed of the woman is Christ Jesus, whom God sent to earth to restore what man had lost due to rebellion.

From the beginning, God had established in Hebrew society that the first born would receive the inheritance of his father, and he would defend and protect his assets and interests. This was not the Israelite's idea, but God's. With this, God established a principle. If the interests and position of a person are compromised, it falls to his first born to take up the fight to restore his honor. As God's only son, Jesus is the only one who can restore the honor that God deserves. He came to announce the Gospel of the Kingdom. What does the Gospel of the

Kingdom mean? That God wants to establish the government of heaven over the lives of men.

Jesus came to restore the position of His Father as the all in all. The process began on the cross, where in the presence of everyone, powers and principalities were put to shame:

> "Having disarmed principalities and powers, He made a public spectacle of them, triumphing over them in it."
>
> Col.2:15

Under the government of God, all powers and principalities were judged in public and condemned to defeat. Under the government of God, my sin debt was paid with the death of an innocent: Jesus.

───────────◆───────────

As God's only son, Jesus is the only one who can restore the honor that God deserves.

However, the process is not yet completed on earth. Yes, Jesus cleared the way for those who love Him to enter the presence of God without making temple sacrifices. But the Father is still at work subduing all enemies under the feet of His Son until the last enemy—death—is destroyed. At that moment, the Son will fulfill His purpose, and God will be the all in all.

Christ came to restore the relationship between God and man. The only possible relationship between God and man is one in which God is the all in all in man's life. This was the original relationship between God and Adam. The first man depended totally on God, who supplied everything he needed. Adam found his delight, his peace, his meaning, his reason for being in God. This relationship was broken when sin entered the picture. Man became the slave of sin, rebellion, his own will, and Lucifer. Jesus achieved total redemption of our lives on the cross. Paul explains it as follows:

> *And you, being dead in your trespasses and the uncircumcision of your flesh, He has made alive together with Him, having forgiven you all trespasses, having wiped out the handwriting of requirements that was against us, which was contrary to us. And He has taken it out of the way, having nailed it to the cross. Having disarmed principalities and powers, He made a public spectacle of them, triumphing over them in it.*
>
> Col. 2:13–15

According to this passage, we were dead. The word "dead" means *separated*. We were separated from God by our own sins, disobedience to the God who should be the all in all in our lives.

There was a "handwriting of requirements"—or bill of particulars—against us. These accusations stood between God and man, blocking communication.

━━━━━━━━━━━ ◆ ━━━━━━━━━━━
Jesus paid the price for our rebellion against the all in all, God.
━━━━━━━━━━━━━━━━━━━━━━━

Jesus paid for our sins. He paid the price for our rebellion against the all in all, God. On the cross, all our sins were forgiven.

Christ blotted out the accusations and disarmed

principalities and powers. Accusations against us were the enemy's chief weapon. When those were wiped out, principalities lost all their legal standing in holding us captive.

Now we are free to submit to the Lordship of God without fear. Now we can enter freely into the relationship that God wants to have with us, because we have a High Priest that brings us into the very presence of the Father.

The High Priest

In the Old Testament, the priests would go through the veil of the temple once a year and they would walk into the Holy of Holies to offer the blood of animals on the altar of sacrifice. This ceremony had to be repeated year after year. But Jesus the high priest cut through the Heavens and came to the Holy of Holies (Hebrews 4). There He presented His own blood, which the Father accepted as eternal payment for our sins. This transaction took place once and is sufficient forever.

This is not a promise with conditions, nor is it a divine suggestion.

After our redemption, the Father tells the Son, "sit at my right hand, until I put your enemies under your feet. (Psalm 110:1) The Father gives His only Son the position that every Jewish first born had: the seat at His right hand. Then He issues this decree: everything that opposes the restoration of God to His place as the all in all will be subdued under the foot of the Son. Everyone who does not confess that God is the all in all will end up under the feet of Jesus. He is the Lord and everything and everyone must submit to Him.

This is not a promise with conditions, nor is it a divine suggestion. It is a decree that is in the process of being fulfilled. And one day its fulfillment will be complete. This is the core purpose of the universe and Satan will try any means to turn the hearts of men against God just to prevent its restoration.

Consider the case of Job. Satan tried to get him to deny God. He attacked Job's family, friends, possessions and health. The Bible states that in all this, "Job did not sin by accusing God of wrongdoing." (Job 1:22) Job complained and questioned God, but he did not sin, and he recognized to the end that He was his redeemer.

Let's see if what was said about Job in Scripture could also be said about us .

The Purity of the Kingdom

Many refer to the affairs of this world as secular and spiritual. In reality, everything is spiritual and everything has to do with God. The key questions are: What place does God occupy in our lives? What place does God have in each situation? What benefit is Satan being handed in the thoughts or behaviors concerning a matter? Is our life worship to God, without reservation, without rivals for our affection toward Him, without doubt and with a whole heart? Is God the all in all?

Is the spirit of Egypt, the spirit of the world, ruling in my life?

Am I trusting God for my finances, health, happiness, future, even food and shelter?

Who or what is leading my life? Am I leading my life? Are my career or goals leading me?

Am I worshiping God totally or do I have idols that are replacing Him?

━━━━━━━━━━━ ✦ ━━━━━━━━━━━
When we mix the things of God with the things of the flesh, there is no fruit.
━━━━━━━━━━━━━━━━━━━━━━━

The core purpose of God is related to everything that surrounds us and is the foundation of the Bible.

God established the Ten Commandments. You can say that that law was for the Jews, and that it belongs to the Old Covenant. However, the Bible says, "And now, Israel, what does the Lord your God require of you, but to fear the Lord your God, to walk in all His ways and to love Him, to serve the Lord your God with all your heart and with all your soul . . . . You shall not plow with an ox and a donkey together. You shall not wear a garment of different sorts, such as wool and linen mixed together. . . . You shall not have in your bag differing weights, a heavy and a light (Deuteronomy 10:12; 22:10,11; 25:13).

In the Law of Moses, God established that, in His Kingdom, there is no compromise. In the government of God, no other rules are accepted but His. It is Satan who mixes the carnal with the spiritual, the good with the evil. God prohibits mixing in His Kingdom. When we mix the spiritual with the carnal, God is not glorified.

The mixing of a horse with a donkey produces a mule. God did not directly create the mule. Man created this mix. Did you know that mules are sterile? When we mix the things of God with the things of the flesh, there is no fruit. In other words, none of the result honors God. The things we produce are barren.

In the laws of sowing and reaping, God establishes that in a specific ground, you cannot combine the planting of two seeds. God even prohibited the mix of materials in cloth. God wanted to establish His government even in the simplest things of life.

In the laws of marriage, God establishes the same principle: there can be no mixing. The unity of the husband and the wife reflects the purity of the relationship of the believer with God.

The laws of the Tabernacle, the priesthood, of the kingdom of Israel, of its monarchy, established the same principles: there can be no mix. God is the center in every one of these laws. He will not share with anyone the throne of authority and absolute Lordship.

In the work of salvation, God establishes the same principle. We have been taught that we are the sole beneficiaries of salvation. However, the core of the work of salvation is that God will establish His position as the absolute center of the life of the believer. Before salvation, Satan had rights over our lives. He was able to accuse us and claim us for the kingdom of death. But after the victory of Jesus, God claims us and separates us for Himself. God is the all in all in our lives.

What is the purpose of evangelization? The core purpose is to announce the establishment of the government, the rule of God in all nations. What is the message? GOD IS THE SOURCE, GOD IS THE KING, AND ONLY GOD IS TO BE WORSHIPED.

What is the purpose of the church? To show the world that God is real and that He is king and Lord of all. It is to show the world a people who submit to the Lordship of God.

What is the purpose of every activity in our churches? To be in communion, spiritual unity. Congregational activities are not to amuse, to raise funds or promote fellowship. When we have communion among brothers, we exalt God, His kingdom and His interests. We do not exalt our interests. That is why Satan hates unity and promotes division. Everything we do should have God at the center. Everything should serve His purpose that He would be all in our lives. Anything that does not will be put under the feet of Jesus.

God has purposed to be the all in all in your life. He should be the center of all your endeavors, thoughts, and plans. He wants to be the center of your heart. If you have accepted Jesus Christ as your Savior, you are free from Egypt and the bondage of sin.

But it is possible that right now you may be walking through a desert in which Satan is tempting you. Maybe you feel desperate to be done with your trial. Maybe you are tempted to do something wrong to try to resolve the situation. Some people, in order to escape a difficult situation move to a new location, get a divorce or take out high interest loans that enslave them. Others use "spiritual" methods, offering sacrifices such as fasting and prayer so that God will get them out of the desert more quickly. We live in a society controlled by the spirit of Egypt.

If that is your situation, stop! Satan has no authority over you, nor is he in control of your desert. But he is still at his chief work of defying the authority of God and trying to establish himself as king in your life. Resist him! God is your all in all.

Can you understand why God is moving mightily in the poorest nations today? It is not because God loves the poor more than the rich or because it is evil to be wealthy. It is because the poorest must make God their source. They cannot rely on riches, wealth, technology and medicine. They must trust God. They cannot trust political leadership, they must be led by the Spirit. They do not want visible idols, they want a living, powerful, miraculous God! This is why God opens the heavens!

I remember conducting a crusade in a large coliseum in Latin America. The day we arrived, the Spirit of God spoke to my heart and instructed me to have a communion service for the Sunday service. I was not sure how we would do it because there was no way to supply bread, juice, and cups for 15,000 people. We finally told the crowd on Friday night to bring their own bread and juice.

Sunday came and over 15,000 showed up ready to have communion. After I spoke about the power of the blood, a blood that speaks, we all raised our cups and drank grape juice. Immediately the Holy Spirit spoke to my heart and told me to call unbelievers to the altar. I had not even explained the plan of salvation. How could I invite the sinners to come forward? Well, I decided to be obedient and before I was done, two men ran from the back of the coliseum and literally dove head-first before the platform. It was like the flood opened. Over three thousand people also followed to accept Jesus as their Savior.

A few weeks later, the coordinator for the crusade called to tell me that the two men that had come to the altar first, were part of a group of Satanists that had been walking around the coliseum, praying incantations and cursing the crusade. The pastor told me that they had felt someone grab them and push them inside the arena. That was the precise moment at which I was making the call, led by the Spirit. Satan was defeated and the Spirit opened the heavens. Thousands were saved that glorious Sunday.

What happened? Was it the anointed preaching? NO! It was the total surrender of the people of God in that city. They had prayed and believed God for souls. They had obeyed and brought bread and juice (even though local pastors were questioning the concept of open communion). They had sacrificed by coming all the way to the arena (even though most of them did not have money for fares) and they worshiped God with total abandonment, with their praise and with their offerings.

God wants to do the same in every home, town, city, and in every life!

2

God's Last and Final Sign

G od will restore His rule on earth as it is in heaven. And He has given us models for how He intends to go about it. One of the most amazing parts of His plan is that it includes, rather than bypasses, flawed human beings.

The greatest sign of the Father's intent to use people in the restoration of His kingdom government is the Son, Jesus. Ephesians 4:7–16 speaks about the work Jesus began to do immediately after His ascension. Once He had finished the work of redemption through the cross, the grave and the heavens, He did not rest but began the next phase.

> *One of the most amazing parts of His plan is that it includes, rather than bypasses, flawed human beings.*

"To each one of us grace was given according to the measure of Christ's gift." Therefore He says: "When He ascended on high, He led captivity captive, and gave gifts to men." (Now this "He ascended"—what does it mean but that He also first descended into the lower parts of the earth? He who descended is also the One who ascended far above all the heavens, that He might fill all things.) "And He Himself gave some to be apostles, some prophets, some evangelists, and some pastors and teachers for the equipping of the saints for the work of ministry, for the edifying of the body of Christ, till we all come to the unity of the faith and of the knowledge of the Son of God, to a perfect man, to the measure of the stature of the fullness of Christ; that we should no longer be children, tossed to and fro and carried about with every wind of doctrine, by the trickery of men, in the cunning craftiness of deceitful plotting but, speaking the truth in love, may grow up in all things into Him who is the head—Christ—from whom the whole body, joined and knit together by what every joint supplies, according to the effective working by which every part does its share, causes growth of the body for the edifying of itself in love."

The "perfect man" is not an individual.
It is the church. It is the body of Christ.

Until God showed me its meaning, I believed that the "perfect man" in v. 13 was a description of the ideal toward which each believer should aim. But this is not the case. The "perfect man" is not an individual. It is the church. It is the body of Christ.

Each believer, without exception, has received by grace something from Christ, as Paul shows here. In this passage, ministry is defined as "edifying of the Body of Christ." (v. 12) Each believer has a place in the ministry.

Traditional religion has taught us that the ministry is only for a few. But the Bible teaches that the ministry is for everyone. We should serve one another so that the Body of Christ may be both edified and protected. The process of preparing each saint and placing him in the proper area of service must continue until "all come to the unity of the faith and the knowledge" of Jesus Christ. (v. 13)

At one level, Jesus is the model for our personal lives. But more importantly for the time in which we live, He is the picture God has set before us of the perfect man He wants His church to be. Paul helps us see the details in this picture:

1. *The whole body, joined and knit together.* "Joined" means "composed, organized, arranged, adjusted." In a wall, the bricks must fit well and be leveled, without any of them sticking out beyond the others. In the same way, all the members of this body must be smoothly and evenly joined.

2. *By what every joint supplies.* As the joints of our bodies keep the bones in their places, the unity of the Spirit in the bond of peace keeps us united to our brothers and sisters in the body.

3. *According to the effectual working by which every part does its share.* "Effect" means "the power to work, efficiency, power, energy." Each member has power according to his responsibility in supplying the needs of the other members.

4. *For the edifying of itself in love.* This is the purpose of everything we have examined so far. "Edifying"

means "to make, to build or to construct." The "building" under construction is the bride of Christ that the Holy Spirit is preparing. There is no point in adorning an unloving bride.

The idea to grapple with here is that God is not preparing many brides. He is preparing a Bride. He is not preparing a group of perfect men, but a perfect man. As individuals, it is vital that we learn to walk, think, and act in unity, faith and intimacy with Christ.

As individuals, it is vital that we learn to walk, think, and act in unity, faith and intimacy with Christ.

You may be thinking "that is impossible!" Not if God has declared it. True, it has never been accomplished at any point in history. The men who have held the positions of apostle, prophet, evangelist, pastor and teacher have not equipped members of the body to the point that they might walk as one perfect man. Individuals want to stand out, to show how they are different. Organizations want to emphasize their "distinctives." May God have mercy on those who have the task of making sure that each saint fits properly into the building that He is preparing.

We are not yet a perfect man. What then must happen? The process must continue until we come to the fullness and stature of Jesus, the model of a perfect man.

What are our signposts in this process? How do we know if we are advancing at all? We must look at Jesus, the sign.

The Sign

The Father declares that His Son will be a sign. "Therefore the Lord Himself shall give you a sign; Behold, a virgin shall conceive and bear a son and shall call His name Emmanuel" (Isaiah 7:14).

What is a sign? A sign is "a mark that is put on or found on things to distinguish them or to set them apart from others; a means of remembering something; a stamp or a mark. It differentiates one place from another. It alerts a traveler to dangers or coming changes. A sign indicates something we are about to see but have not yet seen. It guides to a final destination. A sign signals towards a direction but it is not the final destination.

◆

A sign signals towards a direction but it is not the final destination.

When you go to the airport with plans to travel to another city, first you must go to the airline counter to get a boarding pass. You then leave the counter and head for the boarding area, looking for the sign that will direct you to the gate from which the plane headed for your destination will depart. You find the sign that bears the name of the city for which you are headed. Do you set down your bag, stand before the sign and think that you have arrived? After all, the sign clearly spells the name of your destination. No. This is only the sign. This is not the final destination. To reach it, you must get on the plane and complete the trip.

Jesus was a sign to us. A sign is not fulfilled when it is given, but rather when the thing it indicates actually

31

appears. Jesus was a sign that would, in the future, be manifested as revelation to the Gentiles and glory for Israel. With the birth of Jesus, a sign is given as a confirmation of the hope of salvation. But when Jesus arrived, these things—the opening of the eyes of the Gentiles, the glory of God's people Israel and the salvation of the world—were only hopes in the hearts of men based on promises from the mouth of God.

The Confirmation of the Sign

When Joseph and Mary took the baby Jesus to the temple to present Him, they found there a faithful man named Simeon. In Israel, there was a remnant of Jews, believers who waited for their redeemer, and Simeon was among them. That is why, moved by the Holy Spirit, when he saw the child: "He took Him in his arms, and he blessed God, saying:

> "Lord, now you are letting Your servant depart in peace, according to Your word; For my eyes have seen Your salvation which you have prepared before the face of all peoples, a light to bring revelation to the Gentiles, and the glory of Your people Israel."
>
> Luke 2:28–32

For Simeon, Jesus was the confirming prophetic sign that he had been awaiting. Mary and Joseph, however, continued to be amazed at all that was said about the Child. Especially at the words Simeon had specifically for them:

> *"Simeon blessed them, and said to Mary His mother, 'Behold this Child is destined for the fall and rising of many in Israel, and for a sign which will be spoken against.'"*
>
> Luke 2:34

Jesus was a sign—the sign. But many would reject Him and continue to ask for signs.

During Jesus' adult life, the religious people of the day began to demand that Jesus give them a sign that He was the Messiah:

> *"'Teacher, we want to see a sign from You.' But He answered and said to them, "An evil and adulterous generation seeks after a sign, and no sign will be given it except the sign of the prophet Jonah. For as Jonah was three days and three nights in the belly of the great fish, so will the Son of Man be three days and three nights in the heart of the earth.'"*
>
> Matt. 12:38–40

The Lord's answer was blunt. The only sign they were to receive was that of Jonah—death, burial and resurrection. When God sent Jonah to Ninevah to preach repentance, He had him in the belly of a great fish for three days and three nights. Thus was given the sign of the death and resurrection of Jesus Christ.

The "sign of Jonah" was fulfilled when Jesus died and rose three days afterward. However, the sign of Jesus was not yet fulfilled.

God mentions another sign in the book of Isaiah besides His own Son. He says that all of the children of God would be a sign as well:

*"Here am I and the children whom the Lord has given me!
We are for signs and wonders in Israel from the Lord of hosts,
who dwells in Mount Zion."*

Isaiah 8:18

Jesus was a sign. He pointed to someone who would come after Him to fulfill His work. He was a signal, pointing toward the "perfect man." Jesus pointed to His Body, His Church and her different members.

━━━━━━━━━━━ ◆ ━━━━━━━━━━━

***Thus was given the sign of the death
and resurrection of Jesus Christ.***

How did God plan to raise up this perfect man, so that the sign of Jesus might be completely fulfilled? God is in the process of creating him, still carrying His entire creation toward the day when "the earth will be filled with knowledge of the glory of the Lord" (Habakkuk 2:14).

He reveals something of His timetable in this process in: 1) Genesis and the account of creation and 2) the Law of Moses and the celebration of the established Jewish festivals.

The First Day of Creation and the First Month of the Jewish Year

On the first day, God used "the Word" to create the dust of the earth.

"In the beginning, God created the heavens and the earth."

Genesis 1:1

On that first day, God created the substance that He would later use to form man. Man was formed from the dust of the earth and the breath of God. Therefore, we should not give up if we do not yet see the church walking as the perfect man.

On the first day of creation, God also made light. According to Revelation 1:11 and 2:28, "the beginning" is one of the names of Christ. In the beginning there was light, since Jesus is the light of the world.

***

We should not give up if we do not yet see the church walking as the perfect man.

***

When Jesus was born, the light arrived. The beginning of creation was the sign of the day that Jesus would be born in Bethlehem:

"That was the true Light, which gives light to every man coming into the world."

John 1:9

The basis or beginning of eternal life is salvation, justification, the redemptive work of Jesus. In the law of Moses God established that the Passover should be celebrated at the beginning of the month. This festival symbolized the beginning of a New Year and a new life for Israel. It was passage from slavery to the Promised Land.

The shedding of the blood of the Passover Lamb had to be done at the beginning of the Jewish year. This divine principle—established first as a sign or a type—

was brought to completion when Jesus gave His life, shedding His blood for the redemption of our sins, and the attainment of eternal life.

So it is that God establishes in His Word the primacy of two elements: the light and the blood of Christ. God begins everything with the revelation of the light and the death of His Son.

Three days after Passover, the people of Israel celebrated the festival of the first fruits:

> *"Speak to the children of Israel, and say to them: 'When you come into the land which I give to you, and reap its harvest, then you shall bring a sheaf of the firstfruits of the harvest to the priest.'"*
>
> Leviticus 23:10

Before the harvest, Israel had to bring the first fruits to the Lord for the whole harvest to be blessed. Jesus was crucified on the Jewish Passover. Three days after the Passover, Jesus came out of the tomb as the firstfruit of men and women born to the life of God.

The Third Day of Creation and the Third Month of the Jewish Year

On the third day of creation, God caused the earth to produce vegetation.

> *"Then God said, 'Let the earth bring forth grass, the herb that yields seed, and the fruit tree that yields fruit according to its kind, whose seed is in itself, on the earth.' And it was so."*
>
> Gen. 1:11

In the Law of Moses, God established that the day of Pentecost would be celebrated in the third month of the Jewish year, fifty days after the Passover feast and forty-seven days after the feast of the firstfruit. This was the celebration of thanksgiving for an abundant harvest. Again, God established a sign pointing toward an ultimate destination—in this case, the abundant harvest of souls brought in by the Holy Spirit 50 days after Jesus crucifixion and forty-seven days after His resurrection. On that particular Pentecost, the church of Jesus Christ reaped 3,000 new converts. Since that moment, the church has been reaping souls in every nation.

The Sixth Day of Creation

On the sixth day, God created man to have dominion over all the rest of creation.

> *"Then God said, 'Let Us make man in Our image, according to Our likeness; let them have dominion over the fish of the sea, over the birds of the air, and over the cattle, over all the earth and over every creeping thing that creeps on the earth.'"*
>
> Gen. 1:26

God created man in His image and likeness so that he could be His agent on earth, that he might administer and rule the rest of creation. That was all God's gift by grace to human beings. But it can only be fully realized as we obey the law of God.

The Seventh Day of Creation and the Seventh Month of the Jewish Year

On the seventh day of creation, God rested. In the same way, during the seventh month of the Jewish calendar, God established the celebration of the Feast of Tabernacles, the Feast of Trumpets and the Day of Atonement.

- The Feast of Tabernacles can also be called the Feast of Booths. In this feast, the Israelites had to dwell in tabernacles, or booths, made out of the branches of palm trees and leaves, that they built on the roofs of their houses, on the patios, in the outer courts of the temple and even on the street. In this way, they would remember that they had lived in temporary shelters during the years of wandering in the desert. Everyone was to celebrate the Lord's protection of His people. (Leviticus 23:39–43)

God created man in His image and likeness so that he could be His agent on earth.

- The Feast of Trumpets was a celebration involving the sounding of trumpets calling the people to a holy convocation (Leviticus 23:24). God established the purpose of the trumpets: "And the Lord spoke to Moses saying: 'Make two silver trumpets for yourself; you shall make them of hammered work; you shall use them for calling the congregation and for directing the movement of the camps. When they blow both of them, all the congregation shall gather before you at the door of the tabernacle of meeting.'" (Numbers 10:1–3)

• The Day of Atonement was a solemn celebration that was kept on the tenth day of the seventh month. There was no joy. It was a day of affliction and fasting. Throughout this day, the high priest entered the Holy of Holies with incense and the blood of the lamb that was shed on the sacrificial altar. This was a day of repentance and forgiveness. (Leviticus 23:26–32)

Summary of the Jewish Festivals

If we were to summarize everything we have analyzed with respect to the Jewish festivals, we could arrive at the following understanding:

According to what we have observed, the feasts of the first month—the Passover and firstfruits—were fulfilled in the death and resurrection of Christ. On the first day of creation, God prepared the earth, or the dust, that He would later use to form man.

═══════════◆═══════════
The festivals of the seventh month have not yet been fulfilled!
═══════════════════════

The feast of the third month, the day of Pentecost, was fulfilled when the Spirit was poured over the 120 people present in the upper room and they went out to reap a miraculous harvest of 3,000 souls. In a parallel, on the third day of creation God made plants that would produce seed after their own kind.

The festivals of the seventh month have not yet been fulfilled!

On the seventh day, God will rest and the trumpet will sound. He will call His people so that we can celebrate for seven years, not in tabernacles or booths, but at the wedding of the lamb. There we will sing a new song:

> *"And they sang a new song, saying: 'You are worthy to take the scroll, and to open its seals; for You were slain, and you have redeemed us to God by your blood out of every tribe and tongue and people and nation, and have made us kings and priests to our God and we shall reign on the earth.'"*
>
> Rev. 5:9–10

The Day of Atonement will be fulfilled when Israel passes through a period of affliction and tribulation. In that day of great tribulation they will recognize Jesus, the Lamb of God. Israel will believe in the Messiah and He will forgive and cleanse their rebellion.

But how do we know what period we are in currently? What is our position as Christians?

The Formation of the Perfect Man

We are in the sixth day, the day God created man. This is the time during which He is forming the perfect man. As we wait for the fulfillment of the feast of the Trumpets, the Feast of Tabernacles, and the Day of Atonement, God is perfecting His perfect man, which will be like His Son Jesus.

The perfect man—or the church of Jesus—is being formed "to the measure of the stature of the fullness of

Christ" to resist any deception or "wind of doctrine." This perfect man will follow the truth, "edifying himself in love" for his neighbor. He will grow in every aspect of his relationship with Jesus, who is the head and Lord of his life. He will be established as the body of Christ, helping others and receiving help in any need he may have. This perfect man will be dressed by Christ, in His character and His power.

Perhaps you think I am talking about an imaginary person. But I am not. I am talking about you. You, as a believer and a functioning part of the whole body of Christ, will be perfected until you come into alignment with that perfect man. If at this moment you find yourself crossing the deserts of life, it is because God has taken you out of Egypt (your life of sin) to take you to the Promised Land (to a perfect man made in the image of Christ.)

The Thoughts of Christ

The family and disciples of Jesus continually found themselves confronting the issue that their thoughts, judgments and opinions were contrary to those of the Master. At the wedding in Cana of Galilee, Jesus' own mother said to Him:

> *"They have no wine,"* only to be answered, *"Woman, what does your concern have to do with Me? My hour has not yet come."*

> John 2:3–4

Clearly, Jesus' thoughts were not her thoughts.

I am sure you have asked yourselves the same questions that I ask myself many times. Why do I make so many mistakes in my life? In one way or another I always do or say something wrong. Lord, I never do what You expect of me.

Do you know how the Lord has answered me? "That is exactly what I am teaching you. I cannot go on to the next teaching until you've mastered this one!"

◆

At times, our minds deceive us and we cannot be sure what is motivating us.

At times, our minds deceive us and we cannot be sure what is motivating us. There are times when I have honestly believed that my thoughts and feelings were very holy and Christian, when in reality they contained a high dose of carnality. I have behaved like Peter:

"Lord, are you going to wash my feet?"

"You don't really know what I am doing, but later you will understand."

"You will never wash my feet!"

"If I don't wash you," Jesus told him, "you don't really belong to me."

"Lord, don't wash just my feet. Wash my hands and my head."

John 13:6–9, Contemporary English Version

At first glance, Peter's initial response seems good. But Jesus showed him his error, teaching him to let go of the selfishness driving his thoughts, and led him to the place of reaching for the full blessing of the Master.

The Work of the Holy Spirit

In the midst of the desert, our purest desires and best thoughts are exposed to the deep probing of the Holy Spirit. This will continue until we have reached "the measure of Christ."

The Holy Spirit's objective is for God to become the all in all in our lives. The first lesson He teaches us is that everything we produce, think or plan is the complete opposite of "the measure of the stature of the fullness of Christ." Therefore, our only hope is that the Holy Spirit will do His work in us. If you feel you are not up to this . . . . praise the Lord! You've reached the first level.

At the second level, the Holy Spirit shows us that our model is Jesus. Everything God wants us to have, all that we will do, is contained in Jesus. It is impossible to know God and obtain anything from Him apart from Jesus Christ.

We will never know God in our own strength. He sent the Holy Ghost to reveal to our hearts everything that is contained in the Son. The media of revelation are the difficult situations and experiences in our lives, allowed by God to show us that only the revelation of Christ can help and save us. As we go through these adverse situations, God will show us that, in order for us to become like Jesus, we need a miracle.

Before we enter the desert of the Lord, "we are all like an unclean thing, and all our righteousness is as filthy rags" (Isaiah 64:6). Our only hope is that the Holy Spirit will do His work. Once we find ourselves in the desert, our transformation according to the model of Christ can begin.

Have you ever felt desperate because your life is

not going as planned? Have you felt defeated after trying to please God with all your might? Great! The Holy Spirit has exposed that desperation and feeling of defeat. He can now bring you to a place of total dependence on Him. Don't lose hope. God will finish the work He started.

Jesus could easily see the failings in those around Him. But He never intervened to save His disciples from making mistakes. He allowed each of them to experience doing things their own way. Even during the times that they declared absolute loyalty and faithfulness, He answered:

> *"Do you now believe? Indeed the hour is coming, yes, has now come, that you will be scattered, each to his own, and will leave Me alone. And yet, I am not alone, because the Father is with Me. These things I have spoken to you, that in Me you may have peace. In the world, you will have tribulation, but be of good cheer, I have overcome the world"*
> John 16:31–33

How do you think the disciples felt after Jesus' crucifixion? Surely, a shadow of desperation entered their hearts. But He did nothing to avoid or prevent their betrayal since He knew that they needed to go through that "desert."

The Lord will also allow us to fail. He hears our prayers and our desires to serve and follow Him. He knows our weaknesses and He will allow us to go through deserts to be transformed. Do not be sad, Jesus has already overcome the obstacles that come against you.

If you are ready for your transformation, recognize

that in your own ability you will not be able to produce anything for the glory of God. Leave your defeat behind and say, as Paul did:

"I have been crucified with Christ; it is no longer I who live, but Christ lives in me; and the life which I now live in the flesh, I live by faith in the Son of God, who loved me and gave Himself for me."

Galatians 2:20

You and I are members of the perfect man, made in the image of Christ. But, do we know for sure what our model is like?

━━━━━━━━━ ◆ ━━━━━━━━━
Do we know for sure
what our model is like?
━━━━━━━━━━━━━━━━━━━

3

Jesus, the Model

It is fashionable in the church today to talk about power and position, authority and anointing. It is not as popular to dwell on suffering, submission, humility, and patience.

Yet these are the things Jesus modeled for us during His time on earth. Clearly, He ministered in power and authority. He won final victory over sin and death on behalf of every person past, present, and future. But He did it in the midst of unimaginable suffering. When He willingly took on human form, He put off all the rights that were His as the Son of God. He never once accessed these during His time on earth.

Instead, He accepted a position of total dependence on the Father. This is what He means for us to do—corporately, as the Body of Christ growing up into the full stature of Christ and individually, maturing into fully functioning members of that body.

In every instance of His life, Jesus experienced the power of sin and temptation-full force. At the end, He ascended to heaven, in total triumph over every evil power that confronts human beings.

We must never think that, after His Son attained our salvation and redemption, God will justify us by our good works. He is very protective of the finished work of Jesus on the cross. If Jesus took our place and paid for our sins, how could we think that God would accept our works as payment for his grace? Jesus is the only one in whom the Father is well pleased. (See Isaiah 42:1). If we are to please the Father, it must be done "in Christ Jesus," following His example and allowing Him to mold us according to His model.

Whether passing through glory or adversity, He was showing us the way we were to walk.

Jesus lived on earth for thirty-three years. All that He did and the situations that He faced were signs for us. Whether passing through glory or adversity, He was showing us the way we were to walk. Continually, He pointed to the perfect man that was to come after His departure. That man would be the fulfillment of the sign of Jesus. Let's take a look at how.

Conceived by the Spirit

The Holy Spirit conceived Jesus the same way that He conceived you when you were born again. What God conceives cannot come from man's will or effort. The Holy Spirit is the Spirit of Truth, because He comes from God, and He conceives only what is holy and perfect; He conceives the perfect will of God in us.

Only what has come from the Spirit of Truth will be able to withstand the fire of God's judgment and destroy the devil's temptations, the power of the world and the corruption of the flesh.

When the Holy Spirit brought us to new birth, He made us new creatures according to the model of Jesus Christ. Christ, then, is the firstborn and the believers are brothers conceived after Him:

> *"For whom He foreknew, He also predestined to be conformed to the image of His Son, that He might be the firstborn among many brethren."*
>
> Romans 8:29

Our Position of Innocence

This new man or perfect man is "created according to God in true righteousness and holiness" (Eph. 4:24).

The word righteousness denotes a very powerful idea.

Once arrested and convicted, every criminal must face a judge for sentencing. His position before the judge is one of guilt. But when an accused is found not guilty through the legal process, his position before the judge is one of innocence; he will not be sentenced. He will be granted freedom instantly.

◆

Our birthright as new creatures in the Holy Spirit implies a position of complete innocence and freedom.

Likewise, our birthright as new creatures in the Holy Spirit implies a position of complete innocence and freedom, clear of accusation. We need only grow up into that standing before the Lord.

A baby is already complete in its characteristics at conception. It needs no other members, vital organs, or additional functions. That baby possesses, in its genetic code, all it needs to grow into an adult human being. His genes have all the necessary information to dictate his height, weight, eye and hair color, personality, and even tone of voice. These genes originate with the parents who conceived him. Even before he is born, he is complete. But he needs to grow!

Likewise, consider this: Who conceived you in your new birth? The Holy Spirit. What genes and characteristics did He put in you? Those of Jesus that will cause you to be like Him.

Satan automatically attacks everything conceived by the Holy Spirit. At Jesus birth, he worked through the rage and jealousy of Herod. Today, Satan takes aim at newborn believers. For example, over the last thirty years, we have seen an explosion of conversions in Latin America. Unfortunately, we have also seen that many of new converts do not stay in the church. Numerous evangelistic crusades take place in our countries and they bear much fruit that we cannot retain. Satan tries to destroy the seed that the Holy Spirit puts into these lives. Many times he is successful at it. Generally, the vast majority of people that backslide are new believers. Satan does not give up. That is why we see these people being brought back into the slavery of sin.

God has just confirmed
His will in your life.

Every desire, every vision conceived in your heart by the Spirit of God will come under immediate attack by the same spirit that rose within Herod, that rose within

Pharaoh as he tried to kill baby Moses, the deliverer. Do not be anxious! This is the greatest sign that the Holy Spirit has conceived something within you. When the enemy attacks to kill what the Spirit conceives, rejoice. God has just confirmed His will in your life.

The Journey to Egypt

In the midst of Herod's persecution, an angel visited Joseph, instructing him to escape to Egypt. Why Egypt? Because Jesus was the sign that the prophets announced and which the gospel of Matthew confirms:

> *"When Israel was a child, I loved him, and out of Egypt I have called My son."*

Hosea 11:1

> *"And [he] was there until the death of Herod, that it might be fulfilled which was spoken by the Lord through the prophet saying 'Out of Egypt I have called My Son.'"*

Matt. 2:15

Egypt represents the bondage of sin and the captivity of the world. Every believer, no matter how glorious his experience of salvation was, has to face his old friends, his non-Christian family, and tempting situations. He or she must confront patterns of sin developed in a past without Jesus. God will let us go through those experiences so that we may come out victorious and free from the bondage of sin.

Today there are a lot of Christians who have been in the Lord for many years and yet have not experienced deliverance from the bondage that torments them constantly. How can you tell the world that there is freedom in Christ if you are still bound by behavior, vices and worldly desires? The Father wants you to be healed of your wounds. How can we tell the world about the healing power of Jesus if we are still struggling with wounds of the heart? If your old lifestyle and former temptations still confront you, pay attention. God is taking you out of Egypt to set you free. God wants you to be restored so you can grow in Him.

Part of what God is shaking loose from the Church in the west today is its lingering subjection to a spirit of Egypt. This is in evidence in three ways.

First, our continued demand for visible gods, visible idols. We have such a difficult time trusting God that we trust the church, our leaders, our doctrines, our traditions, and our plans. It is so difficult to trust in the leading of the Holy Spirit. That is why we run to services, to hear prophetic voices, to receive a "word." That is why we would rather operate under majority rule, the will of the people, democracy.

Second, there is a focus and dependence on human leadership. Over and over again, the western church shows a need to link a move of God with certain strong individuals. This stops us from cultivating our ability to hear directly from God and yet, this is precisely His call to us at this time: whole congregations hearing and responding to the voice of God.

Third, too much of the life in the church is based on a "river economy." In the church today, we love the provision and touch of God, as long as it remains predictable and somewhat within our control. The Father will supply! He will neither leave us nor forsake us. We need to be healed of the slave mentality. We can trust the Father. He will lead us to our land of promise.

We need the Lord to get us out of Egypt, as He did with Jesus and His parents.

═══════◆═══════

We need the Lord to get us out of Egypt.

Jesus Returns to Nazareth

After a time in Egypt, God sent Jesus' family to Nazareth with the sole purpose that Jesus might grow up.

> *"And the child grew and became strong in spirit, filled with wisdom; and the grace of God was upon Him."*
>
> Luke 2:40

How normal and natural was this stage of Jesus' life! He returned to Nazareth, a humble, unknown place. So it must be with us. After the initial experiences of victory, propelled by the Holy Spirit, we come face to face with the reality that we must still grow.

Every believer must settle into a congregation to grow in the discipline of the Christian life, no matter how experienced he is or how many people he has brought into the kingdom of heaven. Anyone who does not go through this vital phase, will not grow as he should and will ultimately wash out in his Christian life.

The Bible gives us few details about those years in Nazareth. Though we know little about Jesus' childhood, we are told that He "increased in wisdom and stature and in favor with God and man" (Luke 2:52).

Luke reports the only instance recorded of Jesus' growing years. When He was twelve years old, His parents took Him to Jerusalem to celebrate the Passover, as would all Jews according to the law of Moses:

"When they had finished the days, as they returned, the Boy Jesus lingered behind in Jerusalem. And Joseph and His mother did not know it . . . Now so it was that after three days they found Him in the temple, sitting in the midst of the teachers, both listening to them and asking them questions; And all who heard Him were astonished at His understanding and answers."

Luke 2:43,46-47

When His parents questioned Him about His staying behind, He answered:

"Did you not know that I must be about my Father's business?"

Luke 2:49

Jesus had been in Nazareth growing in the knowledge of the word of God; He was learning "about His Father's business." But He was not learning directly from His Heavenly Father. He probably did not even directly study His Father's written word. After all, no Jewish youth was allowed to read from the Law, the Torah, before age thirteen. So who taught Jesus? Joseph, His dad. Joseph was His teacher. If Jesus was taught and trained by His spiritual authority, how much more do we also need to sit under Bible teachers, especially during seasons of growth.

Every Jewish boy was to be taught a profession or

a line of work. But it was more important to be schooled by His earthly father in the ways of the Lord, according to the divine command:

> *"You shall love the Lord your God with all your heart, with all your soul and with all your strength. And these words which I command you today shall be in your heart. You shall teach them diligently to your children, and shall talk of them when you sit in your house, when you walk by the way, when you lie down and when you rise up. You shall bind them as a sign on your hand, and they shall be as frontlets between your eyes. You shall write them on the doorposts of your house and on your gates."*
>
> Deuteronomy 6:5–9

The boy Jesus was interested in what was most important: the Word of God. That's why He sought the doctors in the law and sat down to listen to them and ask questions. They marveled at His questions. While we are growing, we are to ask questions and learn.

◆
*While we are growing, we are to ask
questions and learn.*

Like Jesus, we must also study the Word of God. We must get into the Bible and take advantage of all the Biblical teaching offered in our churches. We may eventually find the religious experts of our day marveling at our answers to their questions. But to arrive at such a point, we must enroll in God's school and learn under His authority.

Jesus' Submission and Ours

Being a wise child, Jesus was submissive to His parents' authority. "Then He went down with them and came to Nazareth, and was subject to them" (Luke 2:51).

At twelve years old, He was not yet ready to be independent. According to Jewish tradition, He was not yet a man. A Jewish boy became a man at thirteen, so He still had one year to go. Though He was the pure manifestation of God, He was still submissive to the law and traditional custom.

As never before, we are hearing of what God wants to manifest in our lives, in the church and in the nations. We know that He will open the heavens. However, for many of us, the time of full manifestation has not yet arrived. We still must submit to structures established long ago, even while we are aching to live in direct two-way communication with heaven and walk according to directives received directly from the Father. We must not be anxious, for the Lord's day was set from the beginning.

What did Jesus do in Nazareth from the age of thirteen until His public ministry began? We know that He was submitted to His parents. Therefore, He went back to Nazareth to work with Joseph in his wood shop. He had to begin as an apprentice, sweeping the floor, carrying wood, and learning to make furniture. During those years, He worked as a carpenter alongside His father and He learned to do business with the people of the town. He was a carpenter full of wisdom, stature, and favor with God and men.

From the time He was thirteen, after His bar mitzvah, until He was thirty, Jesus was a simple carpenter.

As a boy, adolescent, and adult, He submitted to His parents. We must understand the depths of His humility. He submitted because it was not His heavenly Father's time for His ministry to manifest.

―――――――――◆―――――――――

*We must understand the depths
of His humility.*

―――――――――――――――――

Just as Jesus, God's sign, worked as an apprentice in submission to His father, we must follow His example. After spending time growing and learning the Father's business, the opportunity to serve will come. And we will be able to enter into it in humility and submission, completely free of human pretension.

For Jesus, working in the carpenter shop and in the community, the time of public ministry drew nearer. The day of His manifestation would soon come and the heavens would open over Jesus. But, while He waited, He was submissive to His father Joseph, who did not fully understand his son's true calling.

This is a test through which most men and women of God must pass. How easy it is to submit to authorities who understand and guide us, who understand the purpose of God in our lives. But how hard it is when our authorities do not understand or discern the purpose of God in our lives. But no matter what the nature of our trial, there is only one response: Submit until the day of manifestation comes, the day of open heavens.

God has ordained a specific moment for open heavens in our lives. Just as Jesus went through a testing time and waited, we also must live out our experiences with patience. This is the message for all those waiting for the heavens to open.

In Genesis, God sent Joseph before the descendants of Abraham and tested him when He allowed him to be sold as a slave and be thrown into prison, his feet bound with chains. He suffered in the flesh what the psalmist said:

> *"Until the time that his word came to pass, the word of the Lord tested him."*
>
> Psalm 105:19

Joseph waited and passed the test. When the hour came, the word came to pass. Meanwhile the word of the Lord—the prophetic message that Joseph had received in a dream—tested Him.

Waiting is the most difficult but most necessary work we can bring to cooperating with the purposes of God. Because while God is causing us to wait, He is at work in several other places that we cannot see.

━━━━━━━━━━━◆━━━━━━━━━━━
*God was stirring another
of his key servants*
━━━━━━━━━━━━━━━━━━━━━━━

As Jesus served faithfully in his father's wood shop, God was stirring another of his key servants, the one who would step out and prepare the way.

4

As in the Day of Midian

While Jesus served patiently and humbly in the Nazarene carpenter shop, other preparations for the day of open heavens were underway. The Father was forming the person who would precede His Son into public life and service.

Consistent with patterns He had set long ago, God was raising the prophet—John the Baptist—to send out ahead of His chosen anointed one-Jesus the Christ. Only after the appearance of the prophet is God's Anointed One released. And it is the Anointed who leads the people of God into full alignment with the purposes of God and resulting victory.

The Father knows it is difficult
for us to have patience
when we have no sense of direction.

The Father knows it is difficult for us to have patience when we have no sense of direction. In His mercy, He has established patterns for the working out of His plans, to help us discern between periods of waiting and moments for action. He has also forecast His plans to us, time and time again, through the prophets.

Long before Jesus or John the Baptist were conceived in their mothers' wombs, the prophet Isaiah spoke about the day Jesus would arrive on earth:

> *"The people who walked in darkness have seen a great light; those who dwelt in the land of the shadow of death, upon them a light has shined. You have multiplied the nation and increased its joy; they rejoice before you according to the joy of the harvest, as men rejoice when they divide the spoil. For you have broken the yoke of his burden and the staff of his shoulder, the rod of his oppressor, as in the day of Midian. For every warrior's sandal from the noisy battle, and garments rolled in blood, will be used for burning and fuel of fire. For unto us a Child is born, unto us a Son is given; and the government will be upon His shoulder. And His name will be called Wonderful, Counselor, Mighty God, Everlasting Father, Prince of Peace. Of the increase of His government and peace, there will be no end, upon the throne of David and over His kingdom, to order it and establish it with judgment and justice from that time forward, even forever. The zeal of the Lord of hosts will perform this."*
>
> Isaiah 9:2–7

Though the above passage is a familiar Christmas season reading, the words speak not only of the birth of Christ but of all that Jesus would accomplish from His birth until His ultimate crowning as King and Lord of all.

It speaks of a people in darkness and anguish—Israel living under an oppression brought on by their own faithlessness. But this darkness was not to last forever. The manifestation of the glory of God would fill her "by the way of the sea, beyond the Jordan, in Galilee of the Gentiles." (Isaiah 9:1)

This is an exact prophecy about the appearance of Jesus in the land of Israel—specifically in Galilee, where He lived. A people that walked in darkness saw a great light when Jesus arrived among them.

However, from verse three, the prophecy continues and speaks about the manifestation of the glory of God in Jesus Christ: the multiplying of the nation, the increase in joy for a great harvest, the deliverance from a heavy yoke and the destruction of the rod of an oppressor.

The Destruction of an Oppressor

Did Jesus fulfill this prophecy in his three-and-a-half year ministry on earth? No! This prophecy has not yet been fulfilled. Isaiah was looking even further into the future. He was talking about a Son who would have a limitless kingdom, eternal and peaceful, which He would rule from David's throne.

―――――◆―――――

Isaiah was talking about a Son who would have a limitless kingdom, eternal and peaceful, which He would rule from David's throne.

But, before that kingdom comes, there will be a conflict with the oppressor—"as in the day of Midian." The Prince of Peace will break the yoke, staff, and rod of the oppressor upon His people, and all weapons used in this war will be destroyed in the fire. The Lord will not only reign, but the oppressor will be fully disarmed.

Today, in our time, that battle is underway. The forces of the oppressor, Satan, are, as never before, producing yokes that render humanity helpless to reach God. In response, the Lord Jesus is fighting a battle that will end in the total defeat of Satan. We are living through days of battle for millions and millions of souls throughout the nations. Before Jesus returns to earth to rapture His bride, the church He bought with His blood will defeat Satan and destroy the yokes that now prevent these millions from hearing the gospel of salvation. The heavens will open and multitudes will reach the feet of the Prince of Peace during the last move of the Holy Spirit upon the nations. Have you ever wondered how this will unfold?

As in the Day of Midian

Isaiah states clearly that in that great moment in which the heavens are opened, the enemy will be destroyed "as in the day of Midian." (Isaiah 9:4). The last great victory of the church on earth and the last great revival will be as in the day of Midian.

We will see that there is a correlation between Israel and the church of today and Israel in the time of Jesus. But first we need to go further back and learn about Midian.

After the death of Sarah, Abraham took a wife named Keturah and together they had six sons: Zimran, Jokshan, Medan, Midian, Ishbak, and Shuah (Gen. 25:1–2).

Though they were Abraham's children, Keturah's children did not receive the blessing of the Promised Land. That was Isaac's. The Midianites were descendants of Abraham, but were not sons of promise. They were relatives but they were not true Israelites.

They were also perpetual enemies of Israel. The list

of their sins against Israel was great. Among them was the alliance formed with Moab (Num. 22:4). With the purpose of destroying Israel, they contracted the services of a false prophet named Balaam:

> *"Please come at once, curse this people for me, for they are too mighty for me."*
>
> v. 22:6

This attempt failed but the attacks continued. The Midianites attacked Israel's farmlands. They tried to convert them to idol worship (Numbers 25:1–6). It was then that God gave Moses an order:

> *"Harass the Midianites and attack them; for they harassed you with their schemes by which they seduced you in the matter of Peor, and in the matter of Cozbi, the daughter of a prince of Midian, their sister, which was slain in the day of the plague becuase of Peor."*
>
> Num. 25:17–18

═══════════ ◆ ═══════════
***This command was difficult for Moses
for several reasons.***
═══════════════════════════

This command was difficult for Moses for several reasons. His wife was a Midianite, the Midianites had received him after he fled Egypt, and he lived with them for forty years. In addition, they were descendants of Abraham. Despite this history, the Midianties had lied to the Israelites, enticing them to take their women as wives, and to offer sacrifices and worship to their deity, Baal-Peor. Moses fulfilled the commandment of God and the day it was carried out became known as the day of death.

Then Moses gave all the land of Midian to the tribe of Reuben. It seemed Israel's problems with Midian had come to an end. But it was not so. Years later, though Israel had subjugated Midian, God strengthened the Midianites and used them as a means of discipline.

It's a familiar cycle with Israel: their own disobedience sets them on a course that leads to their own oppression from which God then rescues them. God had ordered Israel to evict all nations occupying the Promised Land. He knew these nations would tempt Israel to worship their gods. But Israel disobeyed and allowed the other nations to live and work in Canaan. And, not to miss an opportunity, they charged them rent for the land.

As a result of this disobedience, these nations became Israel's oppressors. God then had to anoint "judges" to deliver His people. They went through this several times. God raised a judge, Israel enjoyed a time of prosperity and liberty. But little by little, the Israelites would drift back into disobedience and finally into the ultimate disobedience—worshiping the gods of neighboring nations.

So it was that after 40 years of rest, peace and prosperity under the leadership of Deborah, the Israelites disobeyed God's commandments once again. In response, God disciplined them by turning them over to Midian.

Toward the Day of Midian

The Midianites used a devastating strategy against Israel. They would repeatedly destroy their field crops just after planting, thereby cutting off their food supply and preventing them from reaping anything they had sown:

> *"So it was, whenever Israel had sown, Midianites would come up; also Amalekites and the people of the East would come up against them. Then they would encamp against them and destroy the produce of the earth as far as Gaza, and leave no sustenance for Israel, neither sheep nor ox nor donkey. For they would come up with their livestock and their tents, coming in as numerous as locusts; both they and their camels were without number and they would enter the land to destroy it. So Israel was greatly impoverished because of the Midianites, and the children of Israel cried out to the Lord."*
>
> Judges 6:3–6

Once again, Israel waited until she had completely exhausted her own strength to return to God. History repeats itself. She cried out to God but was answered with a sharp word from an unnamed prophet (Judges 6:8–10). Then, because of the cry of the people, God raised the servant who would bring victory—in this case, Gideon.

When we study the story of Gideon, we see a series of traits also evident in the life and ministry of our Lord Jesus Christ.

Gideon and Jesus

1. Gideon lived in an unknown land called Ophrah. Jesus lived in Nazareth, one of the least known towns of Israel. The word *ophrah* means dust.

Gideon came from a poor family of the tribe of Manasseh, one of the least known. He was the youngest in that family (Judges 6:15). Since he was not the eldest, he had no right to take a leadership position. Nevertheless, God chose him because he met the requirements for His work.

2. Gideon protected the food in Ophrah. Jesus protected His call in Israel. We have seen that the Midianites' chief attack on Israel was to steal their food. The angel of the Lord found Gideon hiding in a place normally used for pressing grapes to make wine. Gideon was threshing wheat in order to hide it from the Midianites.

God is looking for people who will not take their gifts, talents, and the call on their lives for granted.

Many had said Gideon was a coward because he was hiding. But in actuality he was jealously protecting his family's food from being stolen. God chose Gideon because he kept the blessing.

God is looking for people who will jealously protect the blessings received through the vision that has been deposited in their hearts and the prophetic word their spirits have received. In other words, He is looking for people who will not take their gifts, talents, and the call on their lives for granted.

3. Gideon repented for the sins of his people. Jesus carried our sin.

Gideon answered the angel of the Lord:

"O my lord, if the Lord is with us, why then has all this happened to us? And where are all His miracles which our fathers told us about, saying, 'Did not the Lord bring us up from Egypt?' But now the Lord has forsaken us and delivered us into the hands of the Midianites."

Judges 6:13

It seems Gideon is blaming God. But the Bible does clearly state that it was the Lord who gave Israel over to the hands of the Midianites, removing His protection due to their disobedience. Gideon was actually confessing the sin of Israel and admitting that the problem was not the Midianites. The problem was really between the God of Israel and His people.

God is also looking for people who are willing to admit their sins, the sins of their people and their nations.

In response to Gideon's confession, the Lord said to him,

"Go in this might of yours, and you shall save Israel from the hand of the Midianites. Have I not sent you?"

v. 14

4. Gideon offered God something of value. Jesus offered His life.

After hearing such a powerful declaration, Gideon said:

"'If now I have found favor in Your sight, then show me a sign that it is You who talk with me. Do not depart from here, I pray, until I come to You and bring out my offering and set it before You.' And He said, 'I will wait

67

> *until you come back.' So Gideon went in and prepared*
> *a young goat, and unleavened bread from an ephah of*
> *flour. The meat he put in a basket, and he put the broth*
> *in a pot; and he brought them out to Him under the*
> *terebinth tree and presented them."*
>
> v.17–19

Gideon's offering was very generous, considering the severe food shortage resulting from the Midianite attacks. Gideon offered a goat, which meant he shed the blood of an animal.

His request for a sign was to ensure that his offering was accepted. Once it was placed on the rock, the angel touched it with his staff and fire consumed it. The fire was a sign of approval that the message of God was for Gideon. God approved the supreme sacrifice of Jesus Christ by sending the fire of the Holy Spirit over the church on the day of Pentecost.

5. Gideon started his ministry in his own home. Jesus also started with those of His house. After this experience of fire and revelation, Gideon received specific instructions. His father had an altar to the god Baal and wooden images of idols. God commanded him to destroy these idols and take an animal from his father's house and sacrifice it on a fire made with the wood from the idols.

    Gideon had to start his ministry of deliverance in his own home. It would probably have been easier in someone else's house. But God, in His wisdom, knew that the first thing that needs to be in order is the home of His anointed one.

6. Gideon confirmed the call. Jesus confirmed His call

in the resurrection from the dead. After the first step toward the day of Midian, Gideon asked God for confirmation:

> *"If You will save Israel by my hand as You have said—look, I shall put a fleece of wool on the threshing floor; if there is dew on the fleece only, and it is dry on all the ground, then I shall know that you will save Israel by my hand, as You have said."*
>
> Judges 6:36–37

Many think that the placing of the fleece meant Gideon doubted, but that is not so. Gideon did not doubt that God had plans to rescue Israel. He wanted to be sure that he was God's chosen instrument.

But the story does not end here. Gideon's ministry was surrounded by a series of events and experiences that ended in the great day of Midian.

God Raises Anointed Prophets

Before every revival, God sends the prophets to prepare the way with the message of repentance. Before the day of Midian, God raised a young man with a message of repentance. Before the day of Jesus, God sent John the Baptist with the purpose of preaching repentance and preparing the way for the Lord Jesus.

In our day and age, before God manifests His salvation, the spirit of prophecy is lifted up in order to proclaim His divine requirements. The purpose of the spirit of prophecy is not only to say that God is going to appear with blessing, deliverance, and revival, but to prepare the way for the manifestation of His glory.

Why do we need restoration? Why do we need deliverance? Because in many areas, we are bound with yokes that hinder us from being the church that Jesus wants. Why do we need revival? Because we need life where death has been.

When the people called out to God, He answered. But before sending deliverance and a deliverer, He sent an anonymous prophet.

━━━━━━━━━ ◆ ━━━━━━━━━
Why do we need revival? Because we need life where death has been.
━━━━━━━━━━━━━━━━━━━━━

In these times of great need, in which the spirit of Midian (Satan) has been consuming our sacrifices and labor, the church starts to cry: "Lord, we need revival. Open the heavens and come to us!"

God has answered today. The spirit of prophecy is rising all over the earth, announcing a powerful revival. The central message of the prophets is:

"Repent! The heavens are about to open!"

We need open heavens because, right now, they are closed. When the children of God cried out to Him during the Midianite siege, He sent a prophet with this message:

"Thus says the Lord God of Israel: 'I brought you up from Egypt and brought you out of the house of bondage; and I delivered you out of the hand of the Egyptians and out of the hand of all who oppressed you, and drove them out before you and gave you their land. Also I said to you, ''I am the

Lord your God; do not fear the gods of the Amorites, in whose land you dwell" But you have not obeyed my voice."

Once the prophet preached the message of repentance, God raised His anointed one:

"Now the Angel of the Lord came and sat under the terebinth tree which was in Ophrah, which belonged to Joash the Abiezrite, while his son Gideon threshed wheat in the winepress, in order to hide it from the Midianites. And the Angel of the Lord appeared to him, and said to him, 'The Lord is with you, you mighty man of valor!'"

The Spirit of Prophecy

The Bible shows us a constant design: Before every manifestation of the glory and power of God, the spirit of prophecy comes onto the scene.

—————————— ◆ ——————————
Before every manifestation of the glory and power of God, the spirit of prophecy comes onto the scene.
————————————————————————

The Lord warned Cain before punishing him:

"If you do well, will you not be accepted? And if you do not do well, sin lies at the door. And its desire is for you, but you should rule over it."

Genesis 4:7

Before the flood, God warned Noah of the destruction of all living creatures (Genesis 6:13).

Before the birth of Isaac, Melchizidek prophesied to Abraham the blessing of the most high God. God advised Abraham that his descendants would be slaves for four hundred years in someone else's land (See Genesis 15:13).

Before the destruction of Sodom and Gormorrah, God said:

> *"Shall I hide from Abraham what I am doing, since Abraham shall surely become a great and mighty nation, and all the nations of the earth shall be blessed in him?"*
>
> Genesis 18:17–18

While Jacob and Esau were still in Rebekah's womb, the spirit of prophecy announced that Jacob, who would be born second and therefore be the youngest, would receive the blessing of his father, Isaac:

> *"Two nations are in your womb, two peoples shall be separated from your body; one people shall be stronger than the other, and the older shall serve the younger."*
>
> Genesis 25:23

Before Joseph became the second most powerful man in Egypt and saved all his family from death, the spirit of prophecy came to him in a dream and announced that he would reign over his brothers (Gen. 37:6–10).

The spirit of prophecy manifested through Joseph several times, warning Egypt's pharaohs about the future (Gen. 40:12–15; 41:26–27).

Before Israel was delivered from Egypt, Moses received that revelation on Mount Horeb.

Before the Israelites took over Canaan, Joshua received instructions regarding the possession (Joshua 1).

During the time of the Judges, Deborah received revelation about the general, Barak, regarding the defeat of the Canaanites (Judges 4:6–7).

Before Gideon defeated the Midianites, the spirit of prophecy spoke, announcing deliverance (Judges 8).

Before Samson was born, his parents received prophetic instructions regarding his call as a judge (Judges 3:7).

After the prophets and anointed ones are deployed, God raises an army.

In the historical books, we see how God warned and directed Israel's kings through prophets. For example, Samuel prophesied to Saul that God had rejected him and selected another king according to his heart (I Samuel 16:13).

The Bible also teaches us that after the prophets and anointed ones are deployed, God raises an army.

God Raises His Army

In the day of Midian, God first sent a prophet to preach repentance. Second, He chose an anointed one. Only then did He separate an army. In Judges 7, we see that God tested thirty-two thousand volunteers in order to select three hundred anointed ones that would fight next to Gideon.

This is a pattern that is repeated in Scripture: The Lord spoke to Abraham, anointed him and gave him descendants. He also spoke to Moses, anointed him and took Israel out of Egypt. God prophesied over the Judges, anointed them and gave them armies to fight their enemies. Samuel prophesied over David, anointed him and God gave him an army.

The same thing happened with Jesus of Nazareth, our sign. As He was submitting and serving in Joseph and Mary's home, John the Baptist arose. God was close to manifesting His glory in His Son Jesus and so the spirit of prophecy had to appear.

Israel's Situation in the Time of Jesus

During the time of Jesus, Israel was still a disobedient and proud people. Though their pride was based on their religion, the heart of the people was far from God. It was then that God allowed the Roman Empire to conquer the land of Israel.

Though their pride was based on their religion, the heart of the people was far from God.

Before the birth of Jesus, Rome set a non-Jewish king over Israel. Herod was an Edomite; he was descended from Esau, brother of Jacob. Just as the Midianites had done, Herod was building his corrupt empire through the sacrifice, work, and taxes he extracted from the people of Israel.

God had issued orders of destruction against Edom, as he had against Midian. But at this point in history, God was using everything as a means of discipline for Israel. And the people cried out to God for deliverance, just as they did in Gideon's day.

It is always God's desire for His people to be free from oppression. He wants us to be free from enemies that would impoverish us physically and spiritually.

What a similar situation we see in the church of Christ today! It may seem as though Satan is winning after all that has been invested: effort, money, sacrifice, talents. We have spent so much money for missions, education, buildings. Add to that the current trend in glamorous conferences. How often I have heard pastors lament over lost sheep who, after sitting under the ministry of the Word of God for a time, have too easily fallen out of fellowship and given themselves over to sinful desires. In my own life, I've had the discouraging experience of ministering in a glorious service or coming away from a particularly special time with the Lord only to fall into an argument with another minister or with my wife. Immediately, I lose the blessing.

The spirit of Midian is alive and active today. It wants to steal our spiritual nourishment, distracting us with unnecessary work or insignificant details.

But the Lord is not ignorant of our needs and afflictions. Into our disappointment, He sends His servant with a message to restore our hope.

John the Baptist Goes into Action

The birth of John was announced clearly. His father, Zacharias, received the following message from God regarding His son:

> *"And he will turn many of the children of Israel to the Lord their God. He will also go before Him in the spirit and power of Elijah 'to turn the hearts of the fathers to the children,'*

*and the disobedient to the wisdom of the just, to make ready
a people prepared for the Lord."*

Luke 1:16–17

John was the son of a priest of a temple of the Lord.
But he did not preach in the temple nor did he conduct
his ministry in a religious setting. Rather, he preached in
the desert, outside the walls of the city. He preached far
from the religious customs of the times and outside the
jurisdiction of the religious leaders who ruled with an
iron hand.

> *John was a street preacher, with no
> church or credentials.*

John did not even dress or speak as the religious
people of his time. He was a street preacher, with no
church or credentials. Humble people accepted John's
message with joy, but the scribes and Pharisees mocked
him, calling him a fanatic and questioning him continually.

While Jesus was still living a private life and preparing for the day of His manifestation, the religious authorities were rejecting John and his message. However, God
would have Jesus' first move into public life be to submit
to that same message.

John's Confrontation

John's message was the same as that of Isaiah:

> *"'Comfort, yes, comfort My people!' says your God. Speak
> comfort to Jerusalem, and cry out to her, that her warfare is*

ended, that her iniquity is pardoned; for she has received from the Lord's hand double for all her sins.' The voice of one crying in the wilderness: 'Prepare the way of the Lord; make straight in the desert a highway for our God. Every valley shall be exalted and every mountain and hill brought low; the crooked places shall be made straight and the rough places smooth; the glory of the Lord shall be revealed, and all flesh shall see it together; for the mouth of the Lord has spoken.' The voice said, 'Cry out!' and he said, 'What shall I cry?' 'All flesh is grass and all its loveliness is like the flower of the field. The grass withers, the flower fades, because the breath of the Lord blows upon it; surely the people are grass. The grass withers, the flower fades, but the word of our God stands forever.'"

Isaiah 40:1–8

Isaiah preached this message to a nation that would go into captivity in Babylon for seventy years. But the day of deliverance did come and Israel returned to their land.

◆

His was the voice in the wilderness that cried out to prepare the way for the Lord.

John the Baptist preached this prophetic message before the appearance of Jesus Christ, in the wilderness, without the clothing or appearance accepted by religious people. His was the voice in the wilderness that cried out to prepare the way for the Lord.

God Himself was preparing the way with His Spirit, lifting all that was low, and bringing down all things that were exalted, making straight those things that were crooked and softening all that was hard.

The spirit of prophecy spoke against human pride, against the flesh and against the empty glory of human works. All these things had to be removed so that the glory of the Lord might be manifested in Israel.

Today, this message is proclaimed by thousands of humble men and women. It is not always received by the religious leaders of our day because a message of repentance and humility cuts to the heart of religious pride, denominational prestige, and institutional achievements. This message requires repentance. But repentance requires an admission of failure.

John preached this confrontational message and, while it was rejected by leaders, people were hungry for the Word of God coming from anointed lips. They went out to the wilderness to listen to John, confess their sins, and then take the step of allowing John to submerge them in the Jordan River before the assembled crowd. This was the preparation for the way of the Lord.

Jesus Approaches John

As John was being dispatched by God to prepare Israel for Jesus' appearance, Jesus Himself continued to work in His father's carpentry shop. God had set a certain day and time for Jesus to manifest His ministry.

Jesus was ready at the age of thirty, not at twenty-nine, not at thirty-one. For a rabbi to be accepted in Israel, he had to be at least twenty-nine. The Father chose thirty for Jesus.

Likewise, the manifestation of the glory of God in

the church is not going to be made in human time or by human effort. God will do that in His time.

Suddenly, without warning or advance notice, Jesus arrived at the Jordan so that John might baptize Him. He had reached the point of maturity and was now ready. When He approached, John did not recognize at first that He was the Son of God. He saw His cousin, Aunt Mary's son.

John Recognizes the Son of God

John knew Jesus in the flesh as a cousin. However, he had received instructions regarding the manifestation of the Messiah:

> *"I did not know Him, but He who sent me to baptize with water said to me, 'Upon whom you see the Spirit descending, and remaining on Him, this is He who baptizes with the Holy Spirit."*
>
> John 1:33

John did not recognize Jesus as the Son of God until he saw open heavens.

John did not recognize Jesus as the Son of God until he saw open heavens. It was then that the spirit acknowledged that He was the Son of God. So when Jesus asked John to baptize Him,

> *"John tried to prevent Him, saying 'I need to be baptized by You, and are You coming to me?'"*
>
> Matthew 3:14

The baptism of John was a step of repentance of sins. He had been preaching to sinners. He knew his cousin Jesus, and he knew He was no sinner; that He needed neither to repent nor be baptized. He knew his cousin was a pious Jew and a righteous man submitted to His parents and the Law of Moses. He knew that He was accepted in His community and had amazed the teachers of the law since He was a boy.

Nevertheless, the day of the manifestation of Jesus had come. God was guiding Him to be baptized and to submit to the ministry of John the Baptist. So Jesus said to John,

"Thus it is fitting for us to fulfill all righteousness."

v. 15

Jesus Submits to John

Jesus submitted to the spirit of prophecy of His day. Even though His ministry was greater, the Son of God or the Sign submitted to an inferior ministry. Jesus did not proclaim His own day of open heavens. He placed Himself under the spiritual authority John, the last prophet of the Old Covenant, and waited for John to recognize Him publicly as the Lamb of God. He who was going to baptize with the Holy Spirit and fire submitted to him who baptized in water. The spirit of Jesus was one of humility and submission.

I have met many well-intentioned men and women who want to be truly used of God. However, when I question them about submission to authority, they claim to be directly under the authority of God. But if Jesus waited for John to recognize Him, we also should wait for spiritual authorities to affirm us, even if they are part of the "Old Covenant" or "Old Guard."

Though John's ministry was only to proclaim, Jesus submitted to it. Jesus could not baptize Himself, so He had to put Himself into the hands of the prophet. Notice that the religious leaders of the day did not do the same.

We saw that before the anointing of the Holy Spirit, Jesus was just John's cousin; in other words, an average person. So, too, are those God is preparing to manifest His glory on earth: average people who will be transformed in God's time.

Jesus' Baptism

Finally, John agrees to baptize Jesus and submerges Him in the Jordan. Luke tells us that this baptism was not secret. Many saw it, and I am sure they saw something beyond the norm.

> *"When all the people were baptized, it came to pass that Jesus also was baptized; and while He prayed, the heaven was opened. And the Holy Spirit descended in bodily form like a dove upon Him, and a voice came from heaven which said, 'You are my beloved Son; in You I am well pleased.'"*
>
> Luke 3:21–22

John saw this event. All his life, he had known Jesus as the son of His aunt Mary. Now he was seeing Him as the Son of God. The sign was undeniable. The

Spirit was upon Him and remained on Him. The prophecy was being fulfilled. The time had come. Heaven was open.

When He was baptized, Jesus descended into the waters of the Jordan. In a figurative way He died and resurrected to a new life in the Spirit. This was a voluntary death and total submission to the will of the Father, the place that the Father chose, on the day that the Father selected and under the ministry for which the Father had anointed Him.

This was a voluntary death and total submission to the will of the Father.

Likewise the Father has appointed the time at which He will send the Church the long awaited revival. But how do we know that the glorious day is near?

Signs of the Last Revival

The spirit of prophecy represented by John the Baptist is evident today. There is a perfect man getting ready to manifest Himself when the day of open heavens arrives. Meanwhile, the spirit of prophecy is rising, not only in prophetic words but also in signs that proclaim the manifestation of the glory of God over the nations.

For example, in the last twenty years, we have seen the Latin American church go through amazing growth. For twenty years we have seen the manifestation of genuine evangelism, deliverance, and anointing in countries like Argentina, Colombia, Brazil, the Dominican Republic, Cuba, Mexico, Panama, Guatemala, El Salvador, and Nicaragua, among others. And during the last ten years we have experienced a dramatic Spirit-led overhaul of our worship.

These awakenings are not what the Bible describes as revival. They have been visitations over cities in which God is anointing ministries, congregations, pastors, and musicians with the purpose of proclaiming that He is at the point of pouring out true revival: open heavens.

Many congregations are experiencing a new and unprecedented visitation of God.

What is happening in the United States, Canada, Great Britain, Australia, are also the manifestations of the spirit of prophecy. Many congregations are experiencing a new and unprecedented visitation of God. Is this revival? NO! It is the Spirit preparing the way for the final revival before the return of Jesus Christ.

Nevertheless, there are many who refuse to accept the spirit of prophecy.

Rejection of the Spirit of Prophecy

Currently, I hear of Christian leaders who do not wish to accept as genuine some of the moves of God around the globe. Instead they spend time looking for flaws, contradictions, or heresy. That is exactly what Israel did in the desert. They did not trust God, nor did they trust His prophet Moses.

Many people go to crusades and special services, traveling hundreds of miles with the hope of receiving a special touch from God. These individuals, hungry for God, have taken severe criticism from other Christians, who insist that there is no need to travel to places where there are awakenings.

For myself, I have decided to submit to any prophetic ministry whose manifestations, though not all perfect, serve to proclaim the coming of the latter revival.

The vast majority of church leaders are cautious and skeptical of these prophetic movements. Many ask: Who are these prophets? Who sends them? What is their agenda? Where did they come from? What credentials do they possess?

I believe that this so-called cautiousness stems from woundedness in the church, inflicted by abuse of the prophetic gifts, which, when misused, caused division and confusion.

While the "perfect man" is quietly and patiently getting ready, the prophetic voices will continue proclaiming. We should actually expect opposition to their message, as this is exactly what happened in the case of John the Baptist. If it happened to the one who prepared the way for the Lord, it will certainly happen to us.

The War of Powers Begins

When Jesus was a child, Satan tried to kill Him through the political system. But after that, Jesus had no further conflict with Satan's powers. Until the moment of His baptism in the Jordan, He had not yet cast out any demons, nor had He healed the sick or done any other miracles.

But on the day of His baptism, Jesus received the power of the Holy Spirit to destroy the works of Satan, to heal the sick, and to raise the dead.

We'll know because we will have to submit to the spirit of prophecy.

When the day of our manifestation arrives, we'll know because we will have to submit to the spirit of prophecy. The Father will demand of us that we die to our flesh—in other words, our will.

The manifestation of the glory of God is near and we must keep preparing.

5

Greater Things and Open Heavens

God will have ultimate victory in the nations through His church. As we saw in the last chapter, that victory will have much in common with Israel's defeat of Midian. Phase One of this final assault on the enemy will begin when the spirit of prophecy is manifested and the message of repentance is preached throughout the church.

This message is exclusively for the people of God. We have disobeyed the Lord as we have adapted to the world and adopted its habits. What is worse, we have allowed these customs to become part of the church. For example, we govern our institutions by majority rule, i.e. "democratically." We treat worship as though it were mere entertainment. We dispense psychological instead of biblical counsel and use the values of the corporate world to measure our success.

In that state, we will feel very uncomfortable as the Lord raises prophetic voices in the church. Their message will focus on repentance.

Such was the message of John the Baptist. Nevertheless, John was not the focus, nor are any of God's prophets. The focus should be on what comes after: the anointed ones whose coming is announced by the prophets.

In John's case, the anointed one was the Messiah. Today's prophets announce the "perfect man."

The victory will come when the church of Jesus demonstrates the power of the Holy Spirit.

God will not raise one man or one ministry to revolutionize the earth. He is raising His church (His perfect man or His body) so that He might reveal His glory to the nations.

The victory will come when the Church of Jesus demonstrates the power of the Holy Spirit and fills the earth with the gospel of the kingdom of God and its accompanying signs and wonders.

Let's look once more at the life of John the Baptist from several different angles.

The Priest and the Messenger

John's father, Zacharias, was a recognized priest and a minister of the old covenant, which was the ecclesiastic order of the times. He was a good man and a faithful worker in the temple, but he had difficulty hearing the voice of God.

The gospel of Luke tells us that Zacharias entered the holy place of the temple of Jerusalem to present an offering of incense.

"According to the custom of the priesthood, his lot fell to burn incense when he went into the temple of the Lord. And

the whole multitude of the people was praying outside at the hour of incense."

Luke 1:9–10

The multitude outside was praying that God would accept the offering. The people were hungry for God and waiting for Zacharias to minister on their behalf.

"Then an angel of the Lord appeared to him, standing on the right side of the altar of incense. And when Zacharias saw him, he was troubled, and fear fell upon him."

Luke 1:11–12

The high priest who had to go into the presence of God on behalf of the people was disturbed when the Lord sent an angelic messenger to tell him that his prayer had been heard.

━━━━━━━━━━━━━━ ✦ ━━━━━━━━━━━━━━

They are upset because the messengers are just too far outside the realm of the normal, customary, and acceptable.

━━━━━━━━━━━━━━━━━━━━━━━━━━━━━━━

Today, there are many men in leadership who have been praying for years for a revival. But when God begins to answer, they are upset because the messengers are just too far outside the realm of the normal, customary, and acceptable.

The angel also gave Zacharias the news that his wife would bear a child whose mission would be to go before God "in the spirit and power of Elijah, *'to turn the hearts of the fathers to the children,'* and the disobedient to the wisdom of the just; to make ready a people prepared for the Lord" (Luke1:17).

The call of John is the same as that of the prophets or forerunners. It is about preparing for the Lord a willing people. The prophets are not, nor should they be, the focus of attention. The attraction is the anointed one who comes when the people are ready. In John's case, the one who was to reveal himself was the perfect man being prepared in Nazareth.

After his encounter with the angel, Zacharias immediately answers:

> *"How shall I know this? For I am an old man, and my wife is well advanced in years."*
>
> Luke 1:18

This priest of the religious order of his day had been praying for a son but when the angel came with a message of hope, he reacted by focusing on his human weaknesses and inabilities. How many of us, though we pray for the move of God, tremble at the responsibility of spreading the gospel throughout the nations? We excuse ourselves because it is an enormous task, requiring a great deal of money and media access.

The angel was quick to respond:

> *"But behold, you will be mute and not able to speak until the day these things take place, because you did not believe my words which will be fulfilled in their own time."*
>
> Luke 1:20

What happened to Zacharias after he had this vision? The people expected that the priest, upon entering the sanctuary would see visions and receive revelation from God.

> *"And the people waited for Zacharias, and marveled that he lingered so long in the temple. But when he came out, he could not speak to them; and they perceived that he had seen a vision in the temple, for he beckoned to them and remained speechless."*
>
> v. 21–22

◆

The people were left hungry, without a word from the Lord, because Zacharias was mute and spoke only in gestures; he could not share the anointed message he had received.

The people were left hungry, without a word from the Lord, because Zacharias was mute and spoke only in gestures; he could not share the anointed message he had received. It is sad that, just like Zacharias, many people who doubt will end up spiritually mute because they do not believe that these are the days in which the heavens are opening. They opt to criticize, argue, and doubt. As a result, they lose the ability to hear the voice of God and are unable to preach His word with power and authority.

Criticizing the Prophet

When John grew up he did not make the same mistake his father did. He did not stay in service at the temple. He was not a priest of the recognized ecclesiastic order, and he decided not to preach within the established religious structure.

The religious people did not hear the voice of God. They were good workers who kept the temple functioning. Sacrifices were offered as the law required. But there was no spirit, revelation, or faith.

On the other hand, John did hear the voice of God and went to preach in the desert. To whom did he preach? To those who had ears to hear. Many stayed in the ecclesiastic system in Jerusalem. They criticized John and called him a fanatic and a mystic. Their hearts were full of fear on hearing of this "new move" and they never went out to hear John preach.

But the people did go to the riverside to hear the voice of God through the prophet. Some followed John as disciples and some returned to Jerusalem unchanged.

John was not perfect, as was the Son of God who had not yet been revealed. In the same way, this move of God on earth is not perfect. It serves only to announce that the manifestation of the "perfect man"—the one being prepared in submission and patience—is near. Let's review once more what the Bible shows about the appearance of the "perfect man."

Seeing the Pattern

John came before the anointed one. As we saw in the previous chapter, God always sends the prophets before the anointed ones. A prophet arose in Israel before Gideon was placed into leadership. Once the prophet announced the message of repentance, God anointed Gideon.

The same thing happened in the case of John the Baptist. After he preached the message of repentance, then the Son of God appeared.

In the day of Midian, in the time of the judges, Gideon appeared. In the days of John the Baptist in the Jordan, Jesus appeared. In our day, we will see the body of Christ as the "Conqueror" that defeats the oppressor and lifts up a redeemed people, who, finally, will be taken up to be with Jesus forever.

We will see the body of Christ as the "Conqueror" that defeats the oppressor and lifts up a redeemed people

---

Using as a basis what we've studied before, let's compare the characteristics of the times of Gideon and Jesus with that of the anointed ones that God will raise in the last days for the final revival:

Humility. Gideon in Ophrah, a town called dust and Jesus in Bethlehem, the house of bread, one of the most humble towns in Israel. The anointed ones that are going to be used these days will be humble, not seeking fame.

Protection. Gideon protected the food that the Midianites stole. Jesus protected His life against sin, resisting the temptations of the devil. The anointed ones will protect with zeal the anointing, the call and the revelation.

Intercession. Gideon interceded for his people in repentance. Jesus interceded for humanity giving His life on the cross. The anointed ones will cry with pain, they will cry and intercede for the sins of the nations.

Offering. Gideon offered sacrifices. And Jesus offered His own life. The anointed ones will sacrifice all things for the sake of the nations.

Testimony. Gideon started in his own house. Jesus came to the rebellious and proud house of Israel. The anointed ones will have a testimony worthy of their families.

Confirmation. Gideon confirmed his call. Jesus confirmed His when He rose from the dead on the third day. The anointed ones will go to the nations with evidence that the Glory of God is with them.

Company. Gideon led an army of three hundred. Jesus chose twelve men to begin the church on earth. The anointed ones do not work alone but as teams, under the government of The Holy Ghost.

━━━━━━━━━◆━━━━━━━━━
There is little time left.
The heavens are starting to open.
━━━━━━━━━━━━━━━━━━

There is little time left. The heavens are starting to open. But, remember, it will happen according to God's timing.

Open Heavens Over the Jordan

A few days after His baptism, Jesus decided to go to Galilee. As He walked through Bethsaida, He came upon Philip, who followed Him. Philip found Nathaniel and told him that he had found the promised Messiah, who came out of Nazareth. Knowing the prophecies that the Messiah was to come from Bethlehem, Nathaniel questioned the validity of this Messiah. Philip then took him to see Jesus.

"Jesus saw Nathaniel coming toward Him, and said of him, 'Behold an Israelite indeed, in whom is no deceit!' Nathaniel said to him, 'How do you know me?' Jesus answered and said to him, 'Before Philip called you, when you were under the fig tree, I saw you.' Nathaniel answered and said to Him, 'Rabbi, You are the Son of God! you are the King of Israel!' Jesus answered and said to him, 'Because I said to you, "I saw you under the fig tree," do you believe? You will see greater things than these.' And He said to him, 'Most assuredly, I say to you, hereafter you shall see heaven open, and the angels of God ascending and descending upon the Son of Man.'"

John 1:47–50

Jacob's vision was coming to pass:

"Then he dreamed, and behold, a ladder was set up on the earth, and its top reached to heaven; and there the angels of God were ascending and descending on it. And behold, the Lord stood above it and said: 'I am the Lord God of Abraham your father and the God of Isaac; the land on which you lie I will give to you and your descendants. . . . And he was afraid and said, 'How awesome is this place! This is none other than the house of God, and this is the gate of heaven! . . . And he called the name of that place Bethel; but the name of that city had been Luz previously."

Genesis 28:12,13,17,19

God showed Jacob a vision of His throne, of His government. Jacob was running from the purpose of God in his life. God opened the heavens for him to see that he had to submit to God's will. Jacob could not run from God's purpose in his life. That's why Jacob called the place Bethel, House of God. The house of God means government of God.

What is the difference between the open heavens in the case of Jacob and those of the Jordan? In Bethel, The Lord was at the top of the ladder. In the Jordan, Jesus was on Earth. In the Jordan, Jesus was one of us, identifying with us in every aspect, ready to experience our wounds and ready to provide healing for us in the cross.

Jesus walked on this planet for three
and a half years under open heavens.

The house of God had descended. The kingdom of God had been manifested. God had come in Christ to reveal Himself to man. The glory of God was being manifested in the light of the presence of Jesus. The power, majesty, grace, mercy, justice, wisdom, and the riches of heaven were being manifested on earth in a man: in Jesus, the Son of God. He would reveal to man the heart, the life, and the power of God. He would reveal to us the heart of God. That's why, from that moment, Jesus began to preach the gospel of the kingdom.

The gospel of the kingdom is not just God's plan to save man from hell. This is only one of the benefits. The gospel is the establishment of God's government on earth. In other words, God wants to establish in our lives His order, so that all creation, all men and women, fulfill the purpose for which they were created.

The heavens opened, and the kingdom of God descended in all its might to inhabit the earth. From that moment, Jesus walked on this planet for three and a half years under open heavens.

Testimonies of Open Heavens

On a given day, Jesus and His disciples went by sea to the land of the Gadarenes. As He came off the boat, a man went to meet Him, bowed at his feet and said: "What have I to do with You, Jesus, Son of God Most High God?" (Luke 8:28).

Some of us would have thought that this man was a follower of Jesus. But Jesus walked under open heavens and the discernment of heaven was available to Him constantly. That is how He knew that the man was possessed. He then used the authority of Heaven and set the man free.

The Bible states that Jesus " . . . had no need that anyone should testify of man, for He knew what was in man" (John 2:25).

Men could not hide their thoughts from Jesus. For example, He knew the thoughts of Simon the Pharisee and saw in him a religious spirit (Luke 7:36–47). On another occasion He rebuked the Pharisees when, in their hearts, they questioned His authority to forgive sins (Mark 2:8).

Nothing was hidden from Jesus because the heavens were open for Him. Jesus did not lose a single battle with

Satan. There was not enough demonic power to defeat Him. There was no incurable sickness for Him. Nature submitted to the Son of God. There was no wind or storm that could stop Him: a fish gave Him money to pay His taxes and a fig tree died at His command.

Knowing this causes me to praise God for sending Jesus. Nevertheless, we know that Jesus was a sign. He was doing all this to point to the perfect man that would come after Him: His church. He promised that His body would see greater things and it would see open heavens (John 1:50–51).

The question is: how can we see greater things and open heavens? Let's go back to the moment when Jesus saw the heart of Nathaniel and described him as "an Israelite indeed, in whom is no deceit" (John 1:47).

Let's remember that Jacob was the first to experience the vision of open heavens. One of the principal characteristics of this man was deceit. He was not an honest man. Furthermore his name means deceit, and his life was characterized by it.

Jacob lied to His brother Esau and took his birthright. Then he lied to his father Isaac in order to extract a blessing. Before his transformation, he lied to his father-in-law. But, after an encounter with God, his name was changed to Israel.

With this in mind, we can see clearly the message of Jesus to Nathaniel. He said that to see open heavens, there can be no deceit (Jacob's spirit); there must be a broken spirit, tested, humble and molded.

The qualities of those who are able to taste and see open heavens have meaning for all of us who hunger to do the same.

For Whom are the Heavens Open?

To this question we can add another: who will walk under open heavens? Those who submit as Jesus submitted:

- He was conceived by the Holy Spirit in the fullness of time.
- He humiliated himself to the utmost by becoming flesh.
- He submitted to His earthly parents.
- He grew and received instruction in the Word of God.
- He went to work as a carpenter though He was wiser than the doctors of the law.
- He waited for the day of Jordan, submitting to His father's agenda for His manifestation.
- He walked totally under open heavens depending on the resources of heaven, the power of the Spirit, and the will of the Father.

━━━━━━━━━━━━━ ◆ ━━━━━━━━━━━━━

The promise of seeing "open heavens" is for those who go through the process of renewal.

The promise of seeing "open heavens" is for those who go through the process of renewal—who leave the ways of a deceitful heart to become true Israelites or children of the promise. A true Israelite is just like Nathaniel, a man with no guile. A true Israelite is a believer who is freed from the spirit of Egypt.

Now, it is important that we see that the heavens opened not only when Jesus was on earth, but again after His ascension. And they can open today.

As in the Day of Pentecost

In these last days, God is raising a great army of believers that will do great works for the kingdom of God as the satanic dominion over millions of lost souls is destroyed. He is raising His "Bethel": the perfect man who will do greater things.

We can know that this is imminent because He is already bringing the spirit of prophecy, which prepares the way for the glorious manifestation of God on earth.

The spirit of prophecy today is telling us of a glorious church that will do greater things. Jesus instructed His disciples to stay in Jerusalem until the promise of the Father came to them. Shortly afterward, on the day of Pentecost, the one hundred and twenty were filled with the Spirit. The heavens opened in that upper room.

The Holy Spirit came upon Jesus as a dove and over the disciples as tongues of fire over their heads. The heavens were open when they went out to talk to a multitude of Jews from different parts of the world. Then Peter preached and three thousand came to the Lord.

The Early Church Under Open Heavens

The early church lived under continual open heavens. Miracles were the norm and believers shared all their goods. There was no room for deceit among them.

God wanted to teach a lesson on the seriousness of open heavens when He struck dead Ananias and Sapphira for bringing deceit into the body.

Under open heavens, the worst enemies turn into the best friends of the gospel.

The church multiplied daily. Steven was stoned under open heavens, as Saul of Tarsus guarded the cloaks of those that did it. That same Saul was later called to be an apostle to the Gentile nations. Under open heavens, the worst enemies turn into the best friends of the gospel.

The apostle Paul ministered constantly under open heavens. Though he may have found himself in a Roman prison, aboard a sinking vessel, or on a desert island, the angels went back and forth from heaven, protecting and caring for him, providing for, and aiding him.

The apostle John was sent to the isle of Patmos, where the Romans would leave the condemned to die. When John came, the heavens were opened over the island. While he was there, God revealed to him all that would happen on earth and heaven.

These men went through God's process. They came to a moment in their lives in which the heavens were opened and they walked like this until the end of their lives. They were imitators of Christ.

What about us?

Open Heavens in the Present

The heavens are opening over our continent! We are experiencing great growth in our churches, but that is not all that God will do. The growth is just a sign that there is more coming. We are also experiencing the manifestation of the supernatural in our churches, but that is not all that God will do. The miracles are signs that point to greater things.

What has happened in the last few years? In the western church there has been a manifestation of the healing of wounded hearts, restoring cold hearts to a passionate relationship to God the Father. In much of the third world, we have been watching a mighty manifestation of the awesome display of the power of God over the power of the enemy. In the persecuted church, we are witnessing that, in spite of threats and impossibilities, the church is experiencing incredible growth.

Look at the signs!
Heavens are opening!

Look at the signs! Heavens are opening!

To the cold-hearted, materialistic, lonely, and affluent western church:

THE FATHER LOVES YOU! HE IS NOT ANGRY! HE WANTS TO HEAL YOU. JUST COME AS YOU ARE, AS A CHILD.

To the insecure, wounded, and attacked third world church:

GOD IS A GREAT BIG GOD! DECEIT, LIES, AND FALSE RELIGIONS WILL NOT STAND BEFORE THE MANI-

*FESTATION OF HIS GLORY. SATAN WILL BOW BE-
FORE THE KING.*

To the persecuted church:

*MAN'S THREATS ARE EMPTY. THE CHURCH WILL
OVERCOME!*

We will see then the perfect man manifest the life
of Christ on earth. Under open heavens, the power and
the authority of God ascend to heaven and come back
to earth. It does not go up and down as Jacob saw it. It
does it in the person of Jesus. It does it over the church
of Christ.

Throughout history we have seen manifestations of
the glory of God in different places and times. The church
around the world has experienced powerful outbreaks
of revival in which the heavens have opened over certain
communities of believers who have gone through God's
process of preparation.

But these revivals have lasted a short time. Every
revival in history has a start and end date. This last
revival will not end. It will usher us in to the conclusion
of church history: the rapture of the saints.

In the coming days we will see, at the same time in
all the nations of the earth, the manifestation of the life
of Jesus through the church. This church will walk in the
supernatural and will not be hindered by distance, lack
of resources, or the seemingly impossible.

The principalities and powers of the air will not be
able to withstand this last manifestation of the glory of
God in the church. Governments and the wise of this
earth will stand in awe, unable to mount any opposition.

Jesus will be glorified and exalted, He will be the head of the church and will direct with all authority. He will be the all in all for her and will govern completely all her affairs.

It is time to move the veil and see the plans of God for the church.

6

The Veil

How glorious is the divine plan for the life of the church! Yes, all these promises are for the Body of Christ. All that God did in Christ was a "sign" for us. The miracles, the manifestations, and the truths that He worked were pointing to a group of men and women that not only would do the same, but that would do greater things.

After the experience of the Jordan, the heavens were opened over the life of Jesus. On that day, the Holy Spirit descended and rested over Him, and the Father spoke and declared to His Son that He was well-pleased.

Before that day, Jesus had not encountered Satan or his demons. Neither had He done any healing miracles. He was only waiting for His Father's will. When the day of the Jordan came, the Spirit came over Jesus and made a dwelling place in Him.

The Holy Spirit took control of the plans and ministry of Jesus to fulfill the redemptive plans of the Father. These declarations seem to conflict with the divine nature of Jesus, who is God Himself, according to John:

"In the beginning was the Word, and the Word was with God, and the Word was God . . . And the Word became flesh,

and dwelt among us, and we beheld His glory, the glory as of the only begotten of the Father, full of grace and truth."

John 1:1,14

Before these declarations it is necessary that we analyze a series of questions and answer them in the light of the Word of God.

First Question

How is it possible that Jesus, God in the flesh, would live the first thirty years waiting for the fullness of the

---

If He was God, why did He need to be filled with the power of the Holy Spirit?

Holy Spirit to fulfill the will of His Father? If He was God, why did He need to be filled with the power of the Holy Spirit?

The apostle Paul gives us the answer:

"Who, being in the form of God, did not consider it robbery to be equal with God, but made Himself of no reputation, taking the form of a bondservant, and coming in the likeness of men. And being found in appearance as a man, He humbled Himself and became obedient to the point of death, even the death of the cross."

Philippians 2:6–8

Before His incarnation, Jesus existed in the form of God. Jesus' essence is divine.

It was not the Father who stripped Jesus of His likeness to God. Jesus made Himself of no reputation "voluntarily." As God, Jesus did not change His divine nature but rather neutralized its effectiveness for the time He was on earth.

In English, the verse is mild—"made Himself of no reputation"—but the original words used to describe Jesus' setting aside His rights have a more aggressive connotation. Look at the way Paul uses the same principle in other passages:

> *"For if those who are of the law are heirs, faith is made void and the promise made of no effect."*
>
> Romans 4:14

Paul said that if the saved, those that have believed in Jesus by faith, still insist on trusting in the justice that comes from the Law of Moses, their faith is made void. The faith in Jesus does not disappear; it is just left with no effect in the life of man.

> *"For Christ did not send me to baptize, but to preach the gospel, not with wisdom of words, lest the cross of Christ should be made of no effect."*
>
> 1 Cor. 1:17

Paul said that if he were only to baptize people or lead impressive discussions and not preach the good news, he'd be canceling out the effect of the cross of Christ in the lives of people. The power of the message does not disappear, but it is rendered powerless in the lives of the hearers of the preaching.

Is it clear what Jesus did with His divinity to prepare for His life as a man? Jesus, being God and having all the attributes of God, rendered useless His divine power. Although His divine nature was in Him, He voided it, cancelled it, rendered it powerless by His own will. That's why, to do the will of the Father and live a holy and perfect life publicly (facing Satan, the world, and, finally, death), He had to be filled with the Holy Spirit.

One question takes us to another. The Bible has answers for us.

Second Question

Why did God become flesh? Why did Jesus take the form of a servant in becoming like a man? Why, after being in

---

♦

And Jesus took the form of a servant
when He voluntarily gave up
His divine nature.

---

the condition of man, did He humble himself to the point of death on the cross?

The author of Hebrews explains it to us in the following way:

> *"But we see Jesus, who was made a little lower than the angels, for the suffering of death crowned with glory and honor, that He, by the grace of God, might taste death for every man.*
>
> *'For it was fitting for Him, for whom are all things and by whom are all things, in bringing many sons to glory, to make the captain of their salvation perfect through sufferings.*

> . . .'*Inasmuch then as the children have partaken of flesh and blood, He Himself likewise shared in the same, that through death He might destroy him who had the power of death, that is, the devil, and release those who through fear of death were all their lifetime subject to bondage."*
>
> Hebrews 2:10,14–15

God became flesh in Jesus to suffer death in our place. And Jesus took the form of a servant when He voluntarily gave up His divine nature.

What is a servant? In the passage in Philippians Paul uses the word "slave," a person who surrenders his own will to that of another person. A slave is devoted to someone else's purpose without considering his own.

Pleasing the Father

Jesus became an absolute slave of the purpose of the Father without relying on His own strength, authority, or influence. From the very beginning, He was predisposed to subject Himself to the Father's plans and purposes. When the moment came for His greatest act of submission, the Holy Spirit was there to facilitate.

Jesus' preparation is seen throughout His first years on earth: protected by angels, He survives the homicide attempt of Herod. He grows up in strength, wisdom, and grace. He submits to his earthly parents. And He waits for the Spirit's timing to go to the Jordan.

In order for Him to remain a servant within the Father's purpose, He would have to depend on someone else, someone who would strengthen, guide, counsel, and protect him. Then He would be ready for the experience at the Jordan.

In the Jordan, Jesus received the fullness of the Spirit in order to be able to comply with the "desire" of the Father, who rejoiced as He saw His Son surrender to His will, dedicated to His plans of redemption and the person of the Holy Spirit. For this reason, the Father couldn't help but be well-pleased. His Son Jesus, the Beloved, was pleasing Him. Now He was ready to fulfill the purposes of His Father. His hour had come! Now He'd walk, talk, and minister in the power of the promise of the Father: the Holy Spirit.

In this crucial moment the heavens opened. The glorious filling of the Holy Spirit in the life of Jesus and the pleasure (total pleasing of the Father) were manifested visually with open heavens.

Everything that happened in Him must
also happen in our lives.

From that day on, Jesus lived with open heavens. In the previous chapter I spoke of the miracles, the victories, and the authority of Jesus under open heavens. But I also said that all that He did was meant to be an example to us. Therefore, everything that happened in Him must also happen in our lives.

Is this a reality in us? It is time to analyze this.

Third Question

We need to ask ourselves now: have we been filled with the Holy Spirit in the same manner that Jesus was? To be filled, Jesus left everything and gave Himself completely to the interests of the Father. Are we today servants of the interests of the kingdom of God? The Father was pleased when Jesus submitted. Is He pleased with our service? Are the heavens open over our lives, and are we seeing the same manifestations in our daily walk?

If we are sincere, we must confess that we fail in the majority of these areas. What is the problem? Why are we not experiencing open heavens over our lives? This is one of the most important purposes of this book.

Sometimes it is that we do not walk as we should, and we do not present our credentials to the world.

The Letters

The apostle Paul said:

> *"Do we begin again to commend ourselves? Or do we need, as some others, epistles of commendation to you or letters of commendation from you? You are our epistle written in our hearts, known and read by all men; clearly you are an epistle of Christ, ministered by us, written not with ink, but by the Spirit of the living God; not on tablets of stone but on tablets of flesh, that is, of the heart."*
>
> 2 Corinthians 3:1–3

═══════════◆═══════════

Paul establishes that a true Christian is in himself a letter or epistle.

═══════════════════════

The apostle Paul speaks of an important subject: How is a Christian to be presented to the world? What makes him different in the eyes of others? Paul does not want to introduce himself with letters of recommendation nor does he need another human being to make a list of his abilities, talents, and achievements. Some people in the church of Corinth had questioned his apostolic authority and possibly asked him for a letter of recommendation.

Paul establishes that a true Christian is in himself a letter or epistle. A letter is a means of communication between two or more people. When someone wanted to communicate a message they would simply send a letter. Thus, we need to keep in mind the following:

1. *Every Christian is a letter.* Paul tells us that we are Christ's letters (2 Corinthians 3:3). The origin of this communication is Christ. He wants to communicate because He has a message to transmit.
2. *Every Christian is a letter sent by Christ.* We are those letters that are written in our hearts. Jesus wants to communicate a message to all men through each Christian.
3. *Every believer is Christ's letter to all men.* The apostle also states that they are to be known and read by all men (2 Corinthians 3:2). The addressee is "all men" and it is obvious that all men should read them.
4. *Every Christian is Christ's letter that all men should read and understand.* Paul says that when men come in contact with the believer, not only should they read the message that Jesus is sending them, but they must understand it. Those who read the letter of Jesus in our hearts will be changed by it.
5. *Every believer is Christ's letter written by the Holy Spirit, convincing whoever reads it.* In this passage we also read that the message that Jesus is sending to all men is written through the Spirit of the living

God. This means that the message has life. What Jesus wants to communicate to all men is not a doctrine or a religion. He wants to communicate life. This message is active, dynamic and effective. That's why it must influence all who have contact with it.

By saying that this message comes from Jesus, and that it is written by the power of the Holy Spirit, we are not necessarily referring to miracles and wonders. The Holy Spirit is powerful because He can convict both the world and Christians of sin. His most glorious power is to convince that Jesus is the only way, the only truth and the only life.

6. *This letter of Christ is printed on our weak and imperfect hearts.* Paul closes saying that this letter is not written in stones like the law of Moses, but in our hearts. The message of the eternal Son of God, which is written by the Spirit of the living God, is printed in hearts of flesh.

When the Bible talks about "flesh" it refers to the humanity or imperfection of man. Therefore, the most powerful message, the one that can transform a human being who hears it, is deposited in weak and imperfect hearts. This is God's specialty. He rejoices in glorifying Himself through our weakness.

In conclusion, Paul said that each Christian possesses, in his heart, a message from Jesus that must be read and understood by all men. This is no ordinary message. It is written with the persuasive power of the Holy Spirit, which is here to convince the world of sin. Yet it is written on our imperfect hearts.

Now, the task is to see if our lives really are open letters.

Here's the Problem!

If it is true that we have in our hearts the message of Jesus, we should be seeing in the life of every believer a steady stream of hundreds of people coming to Christ. Is this what happens? If we are sincere, we must answer "no!"

Paul said:

> *"And we have such trust through Christ toward God. Not that we are sufficient of ourselves to think of anything as being from ourselves; but our sufficiency is from God."*
> 2 Corinthians 3:4–5

Paul is emphatic. We are living epistles, not becoming living letters of Christ or wishing to be letters of Christ. These words must be a reality in which we trust.

◆
These words must be a reality in which we trust.

The apostle adds that God "made us sufficient as ministers of the new covenant, not of the letter but of the Spirit; for the letter kills, but the Spirit gives life" (v. 6).

Paul declares that Christ has made us ministers of His message in our hearts. The word *to minister* means to serve or to give something. This word designates the functions of a waiter in a restaurant. Therefore, the Christian is a waiter who, instead of serving food, serves a message: the powerful letter of Christ to all men.

Are we fulfilling the ministry that God called us to? No! What stops us from carrying it out?

The Analogy of Moses

Paul gives the answer in the next verses. To establish a base, he presents the story of when God told Moses to go to Mount Sinai to receive divine instructions and to write the law.

The people of Israel had just come out of Egypt after four hundred years of slavery. Therefore, they did not know how to govern themselves. God knew that unless the law was given, they probably would perish in the desert on the way to the Promised Land. If the Jewish people died out then redemption would not come through Jesus, a descendant of Judah, one of the tribes of Israel.

For forty days Moses stayed in the presence of the Lord receiving the law. These were moral, ritual, and dietary instructions so that the people could make it through the desert.

The Law of Moses contained eternal revelations like the name of God, aspects about His character, and instruction on how to worship and serve Him. But the most important aspect of the law is that it gave indications, revelations, and instructions regarding the plan of salvation of man through the Messiah, the Redeemer. He would die a horrible death. They would put Him in a tomb with the rich, and He would rise as the king of all creation.

The first time that He revealed himself, God wrote the law in stones and Moses broke it in an outburst of anger as he saw his people worshiping an idol made with their own hands. Then God commanded Moses to go up again and this time He spoke the law as Moses wrote it on stones that He had prepared.

◆

When Moses came down, something marvelous had taken place, something quite outside the norm.

When Moses came down, something marvelous had taken place, something quite outside the norm. What part of the message recorded on Sinai did the people not want to see?

The Veil that Does not Allow us to See

The Bible states that, when Moses came from the mountain, His face glowed for having been in the presence of God. The Israelites could not stand the glory that shone on his face. So they put a veil over his face, covering over the glory.

The apostle Paul narrates:

" . . . *unlike Moses, who put a veil over his face so that the children of Israel could not look steadily at the end of what was passing away. But their minds were blinded. For until this day the same veil remains unlifted in the reading of the Old Testament, because the veil is taken away in Christ.*"

2 Cor. 3:13–14

Paul is saying that the Jews not only could not see the glory on Moses' face due to the veil, but that they still have the same veil when they read the Law of Moses and cannot see the glory of God in Jesus. How sad! Jesus came to His own and they did not recognize Him. The Jews had a veil that did not let them see what God had given them in the law.

The Veil of the Jews

The veil of the Jews was the Law of Moses. Do not forget, they had a slave mentality. They perceived the Lord as a slave master and the law as a set of rules whose violation brought sure punishment. Their belief was that they could satisfy God if they could comply with all the ritual, moral, and dietary details. They were awed when Jesus told them that God would be pleased only if they believed in Him. Religious pride was their veil. Religious pride flows out of a heart that does not know the heart of God. A proud religious heart obeys out of fear.

When Jesus came and the glory of God was bright on His face, the Jews did not see it because they were too busy trying to please God by following the "letter" of the Mosaic Law. They did not worship other gods, and did not sin openly. On the contrary, they prayed three times a day, made offerings, read the scrolls of the law daily, worshiped God in the temple, they dressed modestly and abstained from immoralities. They were perfectly religious! But they could not believe in the Messiah that they were so eagerly waiting for. Their understanding was shadowed.

Did you know that we too could have a veil over the letter that is written in our hearts?

The Veil in Christians

The Jews could not understand what Moses had written in the stones. We don't understand either what Christ is communicating to the whole world through the letter that the Holy Spirit is writing on our hearts. We too have put a veil over the letter that Jesus has placed in our hearts. That's why the world is not convinced when they see us or when they speak to us.

―――――◆―――――
Works are the veil that prevents the heavens from opening over Christian lives and churches.
―――――――

Without a doubt, works are the veil that prevents the heavens from opening over Christian lives and churches. We pray, serve God, and dutifully meet His demands. After years of practice and sacrifice, we come to a place of great self-discipline. We then believe we are pleasing God, and we become proud.

This attitude will bring us to stagnation and empty routine. When the world sees this kind of Christian, they don't want to know Jesus.

When we continually try to produce good works, though they are prescribed by the Bible, we do it in our own strength and not in the Holy Spirit.

How many people are sacrificing every day, praying many hours, and ignoring their own fatigue! There is no glory in this! If you are tired, rest and sleep. Pray when you are rested and can pay attention to the voice of the Spirit.

Also, music, styles of worship, worship leaders, and our own emotions, anxieties, and intellectual positions can be veils that cover true worship. I have seen how someone's personality is a veil and due to it they are dry, hard, strong of character, emotional, etc. Our religious traditions are also a veil.

The Holy Spirit desires to break through in our lives and in our churches, but our traditions and preconceived ideas regarding the way He operates become hindrances, veiling His glory. Paul tells us that God did not want the people of Israel to see the glory in Moses' face because it was a passing glory. God did not want Israel to be exposed to a fading, temporary glory. God wanted Israel to look forward to the "latter glory," the glory of the Father that shone in the face of Jesus.

Today, we have this glory, the very glory that was in Christ. The Holy Spirit hs imprinted the glory of Jesus for everyone to see and witness, but we hide it under veils of religious traditions. How sad! This is the time for the glory to shine without hindrances, without veils, yet we have covered it with veils of our own making.

What is the Solution?

Paul keeps answering our questions:

> *"Nevertheless when one turns to the Lord, the veil is taken away."*
>
> 2 Cor. 3:16

The word *turn* means "to change one thing into another, transform, change of life, etc." This passage states that those with the veil cannot see the glory of Christ, they need to turn and look at the Lord.

Paul is not referring here to Christ. He states clearly that it is the Spirit whom we must behold.

Therefore we must turn and move toward the Holy Spirit, who is also the Lord and who will reveal the light and the glory of the letter that Jesus has put in our hearts. That's why it is the Holy Spirit who is writing it.

Turning to the Spirit

What does it mean to turn to the Spirit? Jesus taught us that He had to leave His attributes and divine privileges, and become a servant, in order for the Sprit to fill, anoint, and guide Him. In the same way, we must leave our human strength, knowledge, routines, spiritual manipulations, preconceived ideas, and even our desire to please God. We must reach the point of understanding that we can do nothing to please God. Our best works are rags before Him.

———————— ✦ ————————

What does it mean to turn to the Spirit?

We have to surrender in total humility and the recognition that we cannot fulfill God's desires. We are totally incompetent. If you think that you know how to pray, worship, and praise, or that you can testify and work in the kingdom of God, stop and turn to the Spirit because you have a veil over your heart. If we think we have a corner on the Holy Sprit because we are part of a denomination or a church that believes in the "full gospel," you have a veil over your heart.

"But we all, with unveiled face, beholding as in a mirror the glory of the Lord, are being transformed into the same image from glory to glory, just as by the Spirit of the Lord."

2 Cor. 3:18

If we recognize our incompetence to pray, worship, and serve God, and we depend on the Spirit, we will see the glory of God face to face. Then there will be no veil, and we will have open heavens.

If every morning we set out dependent on the Spirit as we move through our daily tasks, relationships, and personal struggles, we will see the manifestation of the glory of Christ that is in our hearts. It is very likely that this glory is overshadowed by our very competence in Christian practice. The word of God promises that there is freedom where the Spirit is Lord. Once that liberty is reached, there are no more struggles against the flesh, or temptation, or the world. Now the Spirit is Lord, for we depend on Him totally.

When we turn to the Spirit, He becomes master of our lives the way He did with Jesus and pressed Him to a ministry of glory and power. This pleased the Father and made Him happy toward Jesus.

Pleasing the Father

To please the Father is to be ruled by Him. To please the Father is to hear his voice and obey. Adam and Eve heard His voice in the garden. The breeze in the garden was the Holy Spirit. Jesus heard His Father's voice by submitting to the Spirit. We please our Father by depending on the Holy Spirit.

When God created Adam and Eve, He put them in

Eden. The word Eden means "an amenable and pleasurable place." Therefore, He put Man in the garden of His pleasure. Adam and Eve lived under open heavens and heard the voice of God. "And they heard the sound of the LORD God walking in the garden in the cool of the day"(Gen 3 :8). This expression means in the Hebrew that God spoke to them " in the breeze." In other words, constantly. There were no interruptions in the dialogue.

We please our Father by depending on the Holy Spirit.

This is what the Bible says:

"Out of the ground the LORD God formed every beast of the field and every bird of the air; and brought them to Adam to see what he would call them. And whatever Adam called each living creature, that was its name."

Gen. 2:19

In the Garden of Eden (or of Pleasure) God created the animals and took them to Adam to name them. What a lovely relationship! Then, God created a woman and gave her to man (Gen. 2:22). God as a Father, was showing His loving character to Adam by making him part of His activities. He rejoiced in Adam and Eve.

During three and a half years, Jesus walked filled with the Spirit and always pleasing the Father—all this without accessing His divine attributes. Thus everything He said came to pass. The dead rose, demons left, and sick were healed. No wonder He was followed by all.

Jesus walked in the "pleasure" of the Father. Thus the Father gave Him all authority in heaven and earth.

━━━━━━━━━━━━━ ✦ ━━━━━━━━━━━━━
God is pleased by a life
that is given to the Spirit.
━━━━━━━━━━━━━━━━━━━━━━━━━━━━

One of the most pleasing experiences as parents is playing with our children, especially when we can see that they are enjoying themselves. This happened between God and Adam in Eden. This happens when the heavens are open. God is pleased by a life that is given to the Spirit.

In Essence

In this chapter we've learned:

1. Jesus gave up His divine nature.
2. God became flesh in Jesus to suffer death in our place.
3. The Father's pleasure is manifested in open heavens.
4. Each Christian is a letter of Christ, written by the Spirit on imperfect hearts that will convince its readers.
5. We cannot be true letters of Jesus if we have a religious veil that hinders the view of God's glory in us.

Therefore, what is ahead? God is preparing an army of people, written epistles that will be tested before achieving victories in His name, believers who will be totally dependent on the Holy Spirit.

Here is a simple example of how Jesus did it. Have you ever noticed what Jesus did before a miracle? He always raised His eyes toward heaven, He always prayed, as though He were looking for the go-ahead. Standing before Lazarus' grave, He prayed and waited. He then called Lazarus to come forth. Why? Because He saw the miracle already performed by the Father. The Father had done the miracle, Jesus just called it done by the power of the Holy Spirit. The Holy Spirit wants to show you how the Father is working on your behalf. He wants to open heaven so you can just speak the will of God in any situation and see it done!

7

The Army of God

God will manifest the glory of Jesus in the church in the same way that He brought about victory for Israel on the day of the defeat of the Midianites.

In chapter four we saw that God sent a prophet with a message of repentance. Historically, we have seen that before the glory of God has been manifested in the revival of His Church, He has sent preachers to expose the sins in the body of Christ.

The men and women in whom God chooses to manifest His glory generally seem inadequate for the role.

As we study the revivals in the last centuries, we see the church accepting its disobedience, coldness, and faults. It has been then that great prayer movements have arisen.

After the coming of the prophet God raised an anointed one, Gideon, who protected the food from the Midianites. The Lord always chooses people who have zeal for their call. The chosen are always people who do not trust in their own strength. The men and women in whom God chooses to manifest His glory generally seem inadequate for the role.

After preparing the anointed, He prepares an army, as He did in the case of Gideon.

The Army of Gideon

All the men of war came at the call of the anointed. Gideon wanted to have the biggest and best-prepared army, but God's plans were different. The army was not to fight the battle; God would do it.

The Lord told Gideon:

> *"The people that are with you are too many for Me to give the Midianites into their hands, lest Israel claim glory for itself against Me, saying, 'My own hand has saved me.'"*
>
> Judges 7:2

If God Himself was going to fight, there was no need for human strength, only humble soldiers.

In the last great manifestation of the glory of God over the nations He will use men and women who are like Jesus: humble and dependent on the Holy Spirit. We will not conquer with goods, human resources, or intellect. It will be a conquest of a group, a ministry, or a denomination. It will be God Himself fighting.

Gideon's Army Could not Fear

Those who don't believe the promises of God will not be part of His army.

> *"'Now therefore, proclaim in the hearing of the people, saying, 'Whoever is fearful and afraid, let him turn and depart at*

once from Mount Gilead.' And twenty-two thousand of the
people returned, and ten thousand remained."

Judges 7:3

The army of God will be made of brave men and women of faith that won't set their sight on difficulties. This army that God selects won't tremble before the conquest.

Gideon's Army Passes God's Test

God tests every man and woman according to this text:

"But the Lord said to Gideon, 'The people are still too many; bring them down to the water, and I will test them for you there. Then it will be, that of whom I say to you, "This one shall go with you," the same shall go with you; and of whomever I say to you, "This one shall not go with you," the same shall not go.'"

Judges 7:4

God will see with what desire
we drink of His presence.

The test that God used for Gideon's army was designed for them. I don't want to spiritualize this test. I am not interested in why God chose the ones that licked the water and rejected the ones who kneeled to drink. It is simple. God saw the way they drank. There was a special trait in the way that the chosen drank water. God will prepare an exam specifically for each person and situation. Then He will take us to a place and look at the

127

way we drink. Drink what? God will see with what desire we drink of His presence.

In various congregations on our continent God is manifesting His power and glory. Thousands of people travel to go to these congregations' anointed services. I have heard people say that we should not go to a specific place to look for God. But God will choose those who look for the touch of His presence. God will choose thirsty people. However, here is the principle:

God is not a ridiculous God. But He loves to allow ridiculous things to happen. He just wants to see how we react. If we react with pride, if we are fearful and overly careful, we won't do. I have seen different manifestations of the power and presence of God that scares people, and sometimes it scandalizes others. Many question because they have never seen them before. Well, let us be careful that we do not fail God's exam, which is specifically designed to expose attitudes of the heart that prevent us from being used by Him. He is bringing us to a brook to drink, and we fail because we have never done it in that particular way before. The ridiculous exposes our hearts.

◆

The reality is that we are the last to see these traits in our lives.

You can be sure that God will test your life and that the exam will be different from your neighbor's. He looks within His army for traits such as humility, courage, communion, and vision. The reality is that we are the last to see these traits in our lives. It is through the tests of the Lord (the deserts) that these spiritual qualities become evident in our lives.

God Strengthens Gideon's Army

God knows each of our weaknesses, and gives us the right word at the right time:

> *"It happened on the same night that the Lord said to him, 'Arise, go down against the camp, for I have delivered it into your hand. But if you are afraid to go down, go down to the camp with Purah your servant, and you shall hear what they say; and afterward your hands shall be strengthened to go down against the camp.' Then he went down with Purah his servant to the outpost of the armed men who were in the camp."*
>
> Judges 7:9–11

God knew the human weakness and fear in Gideon's heart. Thus, His words "but if you are afraid . . ." Nevertheless, before the fight with the enemy, God strengthened Gideon, assuring an awesome victory over the enemy.

In the same way, the men and women that will form the army of God won't be super-Christians, but rather those who trust fully in Him. That's why they are sure of the victory before going to war.

Gideon Sees the Glory Before the Battle

When Gideon arrived at the enemy's camp, he heard something extraordinary:

> *"And when Gideon had come, there was a man telling a dream to his companion. He said, 'I have had a dream: To my surprise, a loaf of barley bread tumbled into the camp of Midian; it came to a tent and struck it so that it fell and*

overturned, and the tent collapsed.' Then his companion answered and said, 'This is nothing else but the sword of Gideon the son of Joash, a man of Israel! Into his hand God has delivered Midian and the whole camp.'"

Judges 7:13–14

God had already intervened in the battle before it ever took place. The man that had the dream was a victim of a divine attack. The dream had a crippling effect.

The man saw the manifestation of the glory of God in the form of a cake of barley.

God put terror in the hearts of the army of Midian, invading their minds. The man saw the manifestation of the glory of God in the form of a cake of barley. The spirit of terror that He put in the Midianites looked like a cake of barley that rolled through the camp, destroying the tents. The victory had already been won, though Israel had not fought yet. As far as the Midianites were concerned, the glory of God looked like a cake of barley. It was not barley, it was God! The manifestation of the glory of God looked like a large, rolling cake of barley to the Midianites.

Do you know why the devil is most active today opposing the move of God in the nations? Just like the Midianite soldier, satanic forces know beforehand that the glory of God and victory for his people are approaching. Why is the church the last to see it?

The army of God sees the victory before the battle

takes place. In the Old Testament, we see that the Israelite leaders sent spies before going to conquer territories: Moses sent twelve men to see the land of Canaan, Joshua sent two to spy on Jericho, David also sent spies before going to battle.

In the dispensation of the Holy Spirit, God will send us to spy through dreams and visions. Through visions we will see the blessings and achievements that we will have in Christ—the people that will be saved, delivered, and restored.

In the last years I have had the chance of talking to Christians that have these types of visions. Some have dreams of trips to nations where they will carry out a divine task. Others see the people to whom they will minister salvation. Others see themselves speaking with important people such as the president of a nation. Finally, others see visions in which they pray for the sick and they are healed, or bring someone from the dead and do miracles.

Though there are people who doubt these experiences, God is preparing an army by means of dreams and visions. He will show His spiritual strategy to His army and anointed ones before going to battle. The army of God will go through the nations sure that the victory is of God and, naturally, will give the glory to God.

The Army of God Worships and Exalts the Lord

Before the revelation that he had in the enemy's camp, Gideon could not even offer praise to God.

"And so it was, when Gideon heard the telling of the dream and its interpretation, that he worshiped. He returned to the camp of Israel, and said, 'Arise, for the LORD has delivered the camp of Midian into your hand.'"

Judges 7:15

Gideon saw that God inspired the dream of the Midianite and that He had intervened in the conflict by sending a "cake of barley" in the spiritual realm to confuse the enemy.

That realization caused Gideon to worship God and give him all honor and glory for the deliverance of Israel. When he returned to the camp, he guided the whole army in a service of praise.

Worship is a very powerful tool. The army worshiped because the victory was sure, even if their only confirmation was a prophetic dream received by an enemy soldier. In that spirit of worship they prepared to conquer Midian under the power of God.

What is the enemy declaring today? Powers of this world are declaring that they will reach every individual on earth through the Internet and that man will live a better, more prosperous life through technology. They are declaring that they will cover the earth with human knowledge. Well, we believe that the earth will be covered with the glory of God!

The Army of God Submits to the Orders of the Holy Spirit

Gideon explained to his army, emboldened by the spirit of prophecy, the battle plan:

132

"Then he divided the three hundred men into three companies, and he put a trumpet into every man's hand, with empty pitchers, and torches inside the pitchers. And he said to them, 'Look at me and do likewise; watch, and when I come to the edge of the camp you shall do as I do.'"

Judges 17:16–17

The victory was not the important part, for God had already done it. The important part was how God was going to be glorified, honored, recognized, and exalted in this confrontation. The Holy Spirit is the only one that knows how to exalt Jesus. That's why it is necessary that the army obey His instructions. The men were not there to fight the Midianites, but rather for God to be recognized and exalted.

Today the church of Christ is highly oriented toward achievements for God.

Today the church of Christ is highly oriented toward achievements for God. Nevertheless, that is not its purpose on earth. The key is not the achievements, but rather that:

- God be glorified in our achievement
- God be recognized as the order-giver, who strengthens our hand and gives a vision of His glory
- The achievement may be an offering of praise to the Lord
- What we achieve may be seen as a "work of God"
- Our achievements guide others to worship and recognize His greatness

133

The army of God is careful that all victories are attributed to the Lord.

Obedience to the Spirit's instructions is an act of recognition of God's sovereignty. Obedience to the Spirit is pure worship. God is glorified through people who obey and stay unified under His powerful hand.

The Army of God is United

Now, Gideon's words were to an army that needed to be united more than ever:

> *"When I blow the trumpet, I and all who are with me, then you also blow the trumpets on every side of the whole camp, and say: 'The sword of the Lord and of Gideon.'"*
>
> Judges 7:18

The instructions were specific. The weapons could not be used individually. All together had to blow the trumpets, cry, and break the pitchers. It all had to be done in accord. No one could blow the trumpet alone. The cry had to be one. If the enemy heard one trumpet or saw one flame, with an arrow they could easily kill the soldier that had done it. But God's strategy was clear. He is glorified in the unity of His army. And what weapons the army of God used!

The Army of God Uses Spiritual Weapons

The Spirit of God does not use carnal weapons or human strategies.

"Then the three companies blew the trumpets and broke the pitchers—they held the torches in their left hands and the trumpets in their right hands for blowing—and they cried, 'The sword of the LORD, and of Gideon!'"

Judges 7:20

In this case He used trumpets and lamps. God's instructions to Gideon were clear. He had to attack Midian at night.

The first step was to blow the trumpets. The sound of the trumpets simply woke the enemy up; it did not scare them. The trumpets did not eliminate the darkness nor did they confuse the enemy. It was not enough. Nevertheless, Gideon and the army were willing to wait on God.

Much of the so-called "spiritual warfare" that is done today over cities or nations is just the blowing of the trumpets. This is so dangerous. Why? The sounding of the trumpets wakes the enemy. The enemy hears our shout, and he is warned. Just blowing the trumpet is not enough! Many of today's books on spiritual warfare are simply lessons in trumpet blowing. Many of the prophetic and intercessory efforts being undertaken in our day fail to move beyond the declaration or announcement stage of warfare. And as a result, those involved are woefully unprepared for what happens once the enemy is awakened.

I know. We were involved in just such a situation here in New York City.

October 3, 1998 was our day. We were going to take our city for God. At that time, I was the director of the only full-time Christian Spanish-language radio station in the New York metro area. After much prayer, a group of us felt that God wanted us to gather the intercessors, the prophetic ministries, the worshipers, and anyone who would be bold enough to take the city for Him. The Big Apple! We had invited Marcos Witt, a man of God from Mexico, the most well-known worship minister in Latin America. We had invited many pastors, men, and women of God to help us in this conquest. We were going to blow the trumpet.

By the leading of the Spirit we secured the ground that would be the center of worship and intercession for the day. Randall's Island is in the very heart of the city, just under the Triboro Bridge, which links Manhattan, Bronx, and Queens, three of the city's five boroughs. On this island there was a psychiatric hospital for the mentally insane and a stadium where most of the cults, rock groups, and satanic and new age sects celebrate their events. It seemed ideal.

On the day of the event, twelve churches sent twelve teams of twelve intercessors to twelve key spots of the metro area with anointing oil and shofars, ready to declare the lordship of Jesus Christ, the King of New York. The intercessors of Bay Ridge Christian Center in Brooklyn with their pastor, Dr. Luciano Padilla, Jr. went to the top of the Statue of Liberty to declare that she is not the queen of New York City, Jesus is the King. Other team members were at the bridges-the gates of the city. Some were in the financial district. As each of the twelve groups were praying, interceding, and proclaiming over these places, I would put them on the air, live.

Pastor Frank Almonte of Adonai Christian Center in Queens, along with forty intercessors from the congregation, hired a boat and circled Randall's as they prayed. By noon, over fifteen thousand people had gathered for a powerful time of worship and praise, declaring the victory of God. We blew the shofars and we went home, believing that the city was ours for the taking. But we had stopped short of a crucial step seen in the victory over Midian. The vessels had to be broken! We did not understand this.

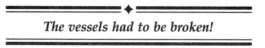

The vessels had to be broken!

The very next week, the most violent criticism arose. Christians began to ridicule us. How dare we "take the city!" They said that we were naïve. How could we think the city belonged to God when it so obviously belonged to Satan. We were shocked. Criticism grew. Opposition came. It was horrible. We were branded heretics and false prophets. We were accused of misleading people in the name of self-aggrandizement. We were threatened with blackballing from within the church and a campaign to ruin the reputations of anyone involved was activated.

When it seemed that it could not get any worse, we received terrible news. Pastor Almonte, returning from a missionary trip to the Dominican Republic was arrested at the airport and held in federal prison, accused by the authorities of trafficking an illegal substance. Pastor Frank had purchased a nutritional supplement for his youngest son that was perfectly legal and commonly used in the Dominican Republic but it contained a steroid that, unbeknownst to him, made it a controlled substance in the United States.

The authorities were very harsh with him and did not follow anything that seemed like standard procedure. He was held without bail in a Manhattan prison and not clearly told what charges were being brought against him. Even more bizarre, after receiving his first visitors, he was whisked away to a federal prison in Philadelphia without notice to family or advocates. He was being threatened with a long prison stay and possible deportation.

We had awakened the enemy. It was time for the vessels to be broken.

We began to pray. We rallied thousands of people in constant intercession. Politicians and leaders called to offer their help. God spoke to us clearly and told us to trust Him. The case hit the news media—English as well as Spanish. They began to report about the situation. We were swamped by reporters—local, national, and international.

It didn't make sense. Finally, the case went before a judge. Over seven thousand believers stood before the Supreme Court of New York building in Queens and prayed for pastor Frank. He was cleared of all charges. But what was God up to?

After the judge's verdict, we all walked out into the steps of the huge court building. Television lights flashed, microphones were everywhere. The media had been recording the actions of the people outside the courtroom. Our wonderful people were praying, singing, and thanking God for the victory.

While this was going on, across town there was another demonstration by other clergy members from the city, protesting the killing of an innocent man. They were disrupting traffic in downtown Manhattan and demanding justice in a very confrontational way. What a contrast to the crowd at the Queens Supreme Court! The Manhattan group was cursing the city instead of blessing it. They were demanding justice with arrogance and threats of violence. They were also breaking the law and were ultimately pulled away from the scene by police.

———————————◆———————————

But a spirit of humility covered the entire demonstration. That's the breaking of the vessels.

While they waited for a decision, the seven thousand people amassed in support of Pastor Frank had been blessing the city and praying for the judge. Yes, an injustice had been done—a man was wrongly imprisoned and denied rights. This man of God was being threatened with further injustice. But a spirit of humility covered the entire demonstration. That's the breaking of the vessels.

As we faced the television cameras, Pastor Frank, smiling, thanked God and the Christian community for their prayers. There was no bitterness. There was only joy.

Pastor Rhadames Fernandez of a Bronx church, El Amanacer de la Esperanza (Dawn of Hope), turned to me and said, "God is speaking to me. We thought that we took the city on October 3rd, but God is showing us that today we have taken territory." All the media was there. One of the city's Spanish language newspapers filled its entire front page the next day with the headline: "Hay poder!" (There's power!) and a photo of Pastor Frank thanking God. The political leadership of the city was begging to be a part of this case, because they wanted to look good.

At Randalls Island, we had blown the trumpets. But

in order to take a city, there must be a breaking of vessels. It is only when the vessels are broken that the fire and the light of God shine. The light confuses the enemy!

It is so easy to do prophetic events. It is so easy to declare and to shout victory. It is not easy to break vessels before the enemy. It is not easy to break whatever is holding back the light of God.

The Army of God is Firm

The army of God obeyed in using the spiritual weapons. That's why "every man stood in his place all around about the camp," to then see how "the whole army ran and cried out and fled" (Judges 7:21).

When they blew the trumpets and broke the vessels that the lights might be seen, the army of Midian went into confusion. The Midianites did not know how to react to this strategy. Never before had they seen a similar attack. But be careful! Here comes the crucial moment. The secret of the army of God is its solidity. It does not conform to the confusion of the enemy. The army stands its ground. Each one must stand, fighting with spiritual weapons until the enemy runs.

God's army is decisive and patient and is not impressed by initial reactions of the enemy. The objective is to drive the enemy to abandon the territory he has taken over in order to then see the task completed.

The Army of God Finishes the Job

The victory was not complete until the kings of Midian were dead. If they stayed alive, they could recruit and return to attack again. Gideon attacked and the enemy fled:

> *"When Zebah and Zalmunna fled, he pursued them; and took the two kings of Midian, Zebah and Zalmunna, and routed the whole army. . . . So Zebah and Zalmunna said, 'Rise yourself, and kill us; for as a man is, so is his strength.' So Gideon arose and killed Zebah and Zalmunna, and took the crescent ornaments that were on their camels' necks."*
>
> Judges 8:12,21

God's strategies are forceful. He did not only want to destroy Midian's army, but all Midian and its kingdoms, kings and princes.

---

*To win we must cut off
the head of the enemy.*

Since the beginning, God established that to win we must cut off the head of the enemy. In Genesis, the Bible prophesies that Satan would bruise the seed of the woman in the heel, but that in return Jesus would bruise his head.

During the years of conquest, God ordered that Amalek be destroyed. When Saul did not obey and saved the king's life, the prophet Samuel cut the king to pieces (1 Samuel 15:33). David knocked down Goliath with a stone, but since he was still living, he cut off the head with the giant's own sword.

God will raise an army that will destroy the territorial armies that control the souls of men. The purpose won't be to "bind " them, but the army will destroy the heads of principalities, powers, and rulers of evil. Without heads, the enemy won't be able to rule the territories.

But, what strategy is the church to use to bring forth God's plans?

God's Strategy

The church of Jesus has been preaching the gospel for almost two thousand years. We have been blowing the trumpet of salvation in a world of darkness. Nevertheless, the preaching of the gospel has served only to awaken the enemy. It has not gotten rid of the darkness. How many times have we seen that when God's love and salvation are preached, other religious cults and pagan religions come to capitalize on the work of the Church!

The secret of Gideon's army was to follow God's plan fully. At the moment of confusion, after the sound of the trumpets, the vessels were broken and the lights were bright in the midst of the night. The fire of the lamps got rid of the darkness. But for them to shine, Gideon's brave men broke their vessels.

The world does not need a more refined gospel, or communication specialists that present Jesus' message with modern techniques. The world needs to see Christians broken before Him and without ambitions, agendas, or pretensions; believers that burn with the fire of the Spirit of the Lord.

The world needs to see in our lives a manifestation of the spirit of holiness, like the Spirit of Christ, who submitted to the will of the Father and became a slave, offering his life unto death. When the world sees broken believers, the darkness will flee from our cities, the heavens will open, the enemy will flee and the army will take the spoils. In the same manner, the church must be prepared as an army prepares for battle.

The Preparation of the Army

We must stop here for a moment, now that we've reached a crucial point. How does this army prepare to walk under open heavens? What practical steps can you begin to take to see open heavens in your life? The answer is simple: God will take us to the place of repentance, a place of brokenness.

In chapter 3, I spoke of Jesus as the model. In talking about Jesus, the Bible states:

"Though He was a Son, yet He learned obedience by the things which He suffered. And having been perfected, He became the author of eternal salvation to all that obey Him."

Heb 5:8–9

Jesus learned obedience through a series of trials during the process of perfecting. This does not mean that He was imperfect or weak in any area of His life, or that He had to better His character. This means only that He matured gradually in the will of the Father.

Jesus gave up the privilege of knowing the details of the redemption plan and surrendered to the Father, depending on His minute-to-minute guidance. Though He could have known all that was in the Father's plans, He gave His future over to the hands of the Spirit, who followed Him from birth until ascension. The secret of the life of Jesus was the total obedience to the Father.

How can we reach that state when we are rebellious, sinful, and selfish? The Father has a plan for each of us: He sent the Spirit to produce the character of Jesus in us. To achieve this, what must we do? First, know that God wants to keep open heavens.

The Cry of Isaiah and God's Answer

During Isaiah's days, Israel was going through tough moments, since they had forgotten about God and attempted to serve Him as it pleased them. Even though the priests made sure that all rituals were met, Isaiah lifts this cry:

> *"Look down from heaven, and see from your habitation, holy and glorious. Where are Your zeal and Your strength, the yearning of Your heart and Your mercies toward me? Are they restrained? Doubtless You are our Father, though Abraham was ignorant of us, and Israel does not acknowledge us. You, O Lord, are our Father; our Redeemer from everlasting is Your name."*
>
> Isaiah 63:15–16

◆

When he saw the present lack of moral and spiritual fiber, he asked himself when God would act.

Isaiah was frustrated. He had a vision of the glory of God in which he was sent to preach restoration and grace. But when he saw the present lack of moral and spiritual fiber, he asked himself when God would act. As he saw Israel go from bad to worse, He asked God how long He would allow this spiritual disaster. What's worse is that Isaiah had seen Israel's destiny in captivity. That's why he cries:

> *"Oh, that You would rend the heavens! That You would come down! That the mountains might shake at Your presence— as fire burns brushwood, as fire causes water to boil-to make Your name known to Your adversaries, that the nations may tremble at Your presence."*
>
> Isaiah 64:1–2

This is the prayer of a God-fearing man who asks for open heavens in the manifestation of the glory of God as fire. God answers:

> *"I was sought by those who did not ask for Me; I was found by those who did not seek Me. I said 'Here I am, here I am,' to a nation that was not called by my name."*
>
> Isaiah 65:1

What an answer! God tells Isaiah not to ask for open heavens, since He had never abandoned His people. It was the people who abandoned Him. The hearts of the people were closed, not the heavens. The heavens were not brass but rather the hearts.

We can paraphrase the word of God: "I've always been here, but I was found by those that did not know how to find Me or talk to Me. Those that knew how to find Me and talk to Me did not find me."

The religious Jews were very strict in their devotion to God, but their hearts were far and did not hear the voice. Then the Lord had to raise others: the Gentiles that answer the invitation of God. Is this not the current situation? Many Christians who have known Jesus for years are not seeing open heavens. Nevertheless, there are new believers that without knowing much are seeing manifestations of glory and power.

━━━━━━━━━━◆━━━━━━━━━━

He wants to show us what hinders us
from enjoying open heavens.

━━━━━━━━━━━━━━━━━━━━

We must heed the voice of the Spirit that calls us to repentance and wants to teach us to be like Jesus. He wants to show us what hinders us from enjoying open heavens.

The True Problems of the People

What were Israel's problems in the days of Isaiah? In this chapter God gives the prophet a list of things that separate the people from Him.

Rebellion

God rebukes evil, for He cannot overlook it. Nor will He overlook those that go their sinful ways:

> *"I have stretched out My hands all day long to a rebellious people, who walk in a way that is not good, according to their own thoughts"*
>
> (Isaiah 65:2).

God does not tell us that the people are rebellious because they disobey His word, but rather that they walk in their own ways.

Today we want to follow God according to concepts that we have created by human traditions; we interpret the spiritual truths according to our understanding; and we construct doctrines and dogmas, presenting them as if they were God's. To God, this is rebellion. A rebellious heart is not a worshiping heart.

Impure Worship

God confronts Israel for their idolatry and pagan practices:

> *"A people who provoke Me to anger continually to my face; who sacrifice in gardens, and burn incense on altars of brick."*
> Isaiah 65:3

God established that worship should be as He directed. In the times of Isaiah, Israel had to worship in the temple of Jerusalem. Due to their lack of fear of God, the Israelites found easier ways of worshiping. That's why the prophet talks of sacrifices that were presented in gardens.

God did not accept the altars in the gardens, though they may have been more beautiful and better prepared. Nor did He want the incense worship to be done on bricks. Men made the bricks. God had established that the altars had to be of natural rocks, and not formed with hammer and chisel. Israel was offering the incense of prayer over structures made by men, and that's why the Lord did not accept their prayers.

In the era of the Spirit, the worship that God accepts is " in spirit and Truth." It is in Spirit, because the Holy Spirit guides from our spirit to God's heart. It is in the Spirit for it is not in our flesh or strength. It is in truth, for it must be genuine, based in the Word of God.

The worship of the church must not be based only

on tradition, human emotion, culture, or popular style that becomes routine. God does not want us to sacrifice in "gardens" at our convenience but rather to sacrifice worship at altars that please Him.

God's altars are places of death and sacrifice. Here the only thing to be exalted is God and the flesh must die (personal desires, works, and ego). We must learn to worship as it pleases Him.

Ignorance

The people of Israel behaved ignorantly, and their worship was empty.

> *"Who sit among the graves and spend the night in the tombs."*
>
> Isaiah 65:4

When we don't worship as He demands, the life of the Spirit is not imparted. When the life, the power, and the anointing of the Spirit are not manifested in the life of a Christian, it is as if he or she lived in darkness. The soul is sad. How is this reflected?

═══════════ ✦ ═══════════
The people of Israel behaved ignorantly, and their worship was empty.
═══════════════════════════

Abominations

The life of someone in darkness is full of abominations:

> *"Who eat swine's flesh, and the broth of abominable things is in their vessels."*
>
> Isaiah 65:4

148

The Israelites of that time did not eat pork nor any impure animal, so God was not talking about food. Let's recall Jesus' words:

> *"Not what goes into the mouth defiles a man; but what comes out of the mouth, this defiles a man."*
>
> Mathew 15:11

The people of Israel did not eat pork for it was not a ruminant, though it had a hoof. With the hoof, the animals can select the food that they are going to eat, breaking it and cleaning it from other elements. Ruminant animals chew their food and bring it back to then consume it again.

After the ruminant process, only the food that will be consumed is left. Sheep, for example, swallow grass, rocks, and other elements that cannot be digested. But after going over the ruminant process various times, they cast out what is not digestible.

This is very similar to a Christian who does not care what he absorbs. His outward form has all the right elements, but inwardly he is absorbing concepts that are carnal, worldly, and religious.

Religious Pride

Even in this perverse situation that they were in, they thought that they were more holy than anyone else.

> *"Who say, 'Keep to yourself, do not come near me, for I am holier than you!' These are smoke in My nostrils, a fire that burns all the day."*
>
> Isaiah 65:5

Those words must not come from a Christian mouth. Nevertheless, we hear them in the mouths of Christians that think they are better than others are. These words come out of a heart that is following the rituals but is far from the heart of God.

It is necessary that the people rise up and recognize their sin. We must humble ourselves before God if we want open heavens.

In Prayer and Supplication

God did not close the heavens nor does He want to. It is we who have closed our hearts to the Spirit due to our rebellion, hard hearts, and pride. The message of the spirit of prophecy through the prophets that will rise in the last days will be to repent of all evil within the church. That's why it is important that we stay in prayer as did the disciples after Jesus ascended.

The Fifty Days

In the book of Acts we see what happened in the days before Pentecost. Jesus told the disciples to stay in Jerusalem.

> *"And being assembled together with them, He commanded them not to depart from Jerusalem, but to wait for the Promise of the Father, 'which,' He said, 'you have heard from Me.'"*
>
> Acts 1:4

Jesus was crucified during the Passover feast. Fifty days after Passover, the Jews celebrate Pentecost, and it is called also the feast of the first fruits. The Bible tells us that after His death, Jesus was in the tomb for three days; so there were forty-seven days until Pentecost.

━━━━━━━━━━━━━━━ ✦ ━━━━━━━━━━━━━━━

They were in communion with God
and studied the Word.

━━━━━━━━━━━━━━━━━━━━━━━━━━━━━━━

After His resurrection, Jesus appeared to the apostles for forty days and spoke to them about the kingdom of God (Acts 1:3). Before His ascension He commanded them to stay in Jerusalem. There were then seven days until Pentecost, and He told them to wait in Jerusalem. What, then did the followers of Jesus do during the seven days before the coming of the Spirit?

> *"These all continued with one accord in prayer and supplication, with the women and Mary the mother of Jesus, and with His brothers."*
>
> Acts 1:14

All of them were praying and crying. They were in communion with God and studied the Word. In Acts 1:15–17, Peter reminds the one hundred and twenty gathered of the prophecies concerning Judas.

> *"And in those days Peter stood up in the midst of the disciples (altogether the number of names was about a hundred and twenty), and said, 'Men and brethren, this Scripture had to be fulfilled, which the Holy Spirit spoke before by the mouth of David concerning Judas, who became a guide to those who arrested Jesus; for he was numbered with us and obtained a part in this ministry."*
>
> Acts 1:15–17

As they stayed in Jerusalem praying, the Spirit led the disciples to repentance. The first one hundred and twenty in the church had a problem that had to be resolved before the coming of the Holy Spirit: the bad testimony of Judas. Not only did he sell Jesus but, with the money, the religious leaders bought a field to bury foreigners. In that very field he later committed suicide.

Judas was the one who betrayed Jesus. His betrayal earned him thirty pieces of silver. When he realized what he had done, Judas returned the money to the religious leaders that hired him. They did not want to keep the money, so they purchased a piece of land to bury the foreigners, the unclean, non-Jews that could not be buried in Jewish cemeteries. What a shameful thing! What an embarrassment to the disciples, to the cause of Jesus!

> *"And it became known to all those dwelling in Jerusalem; so that field is called in their own language, Akel Dama, that is, Field of Blood."*
>
> Acts 1:19

Peter took the responsibility of taking Judas' case before the group and asked for suggestions of how to heal the situation. Before the coming of the Spirit the church had to deal with the case of Judas, his empty spot and the acknowledgement of his sin and its consequences, an unclean field of blood for a testimony.

The Recognition of Our Sins

To fix the case, they acknowledged the betrayal of Judas and selected Matthias, a true witness of the Lord to take his place.

On the day of Pentecost the heavens would open over the one hundred and twenty and the Spirit would fill them, as it happened with Jesus on the day of His baptism in the Jordan. But there could not be any blemish in the church. There could not be a sin of blood. The one hundred and twenty repented in prayer and weeping. They took steps to fix the problem and prepare themselves to see open heavens.

Today, as a Christian community, we have left public "fields of blood," and we've not shown Christian love. Throughout history, the church has spilled blood to defend theological positions, political interests, and revenge. We've fought for doctrinal stands, and we have shamed the cause of the gospel.

***

The army that God is raising in the earth has a sure victory.

The army that God is raising on the earth has a sure victory because it will move with open heavens from family to family, town to town, city to city, and nation to nation. The glory of God will go forth and destroy the enemy as in the day of Midian, but before this, the prophets will rise up to cry that today is the moment of repentance.

God never wanted to close the heavens. Nor does He want to close the heavens today. Thus, these are times of reflection in which we must allow the Holy Spirit to tell us how we have left the heart of God.

In Essence

God is raising among His people an army that will recognize sin in the church and will call them to repentance.

That army will:

1. Be brave and humble
2. Pass God's exam
3. Have God's strength
4. Have God's victory before the battle
5. Worship and praise God
6. Submit to the orders of the Holy Spirit
7. Be united and firm
8. Finish the task
9. Use spiritual weapons

As in the army of Gideon, the chosen will be people who can identify the voice of the Father so that they can carry out His orders.

8

The Voice of the Father

G od takes us from a life of sin and death and brings us to a life of victory and glory. In the first chapter, I spoke of the direction that the Christian takes after being born again.

God took the Israelites out of Egypt to take them to the Promised Land. His will was not only to deliver them from bondage, but also to introduce them to the land of promise that was the inheritance of Israel.

In the same way, God does not save us only to deliver us from sin and hell. His will is that we all go into His inheritance—that is, the fulfillment of His promises and purposes. He wants all believers to live under open heavens. In other words, filled with the Holy Spirit, hearing the voice of the Father, and living in communion with Him.

---◆---

God the Father is the source
of all that we need.

In Chapter two, I spoke about God's purpose in our lives. There is no doubt that He wants us to depend on Him and have Him as the all in all of our lives. God the Father is the source of all that we need. He is the One who opens the heavens and supplies all blessings, offers all direction and revelation, the One who executes each miracle.

Israel went through a desert, or a time of examination, for forty years between Egypt and Canaan. In that time, God revealed His purpose: He wanted to be the all in all for His people.

Throughout the years in the desert, Israel had water to drink, manna and meat to eat, and protection against the weather. God was their healer and provider, but most important, God was revealing His will through Moses the prophet.

Jesus went through the same experience. God sent Him with a promise: He'd be the savior, light of revelation to the Gentiles, Glory of Israel, King over the throne of David, and Emanuel, God with us.

Jesus was the fulfillment of the promise of salvation that came to open the heavens for all who believe. God reconciled with the world through Him. When Jesus executed the will of the Father on the cross, paying for our sins and offering His blood in exchange for our salvation, the Father sent the Spirit and opened the heavens. Not only for Israel but for all flesh, for all men. Nevertheless, in the period between the promise and its fulfillment, Jesus had to go through a desert of disciplines.

In Chapters 3 and 4, I spoke about the life of Jesus. He waited and was tried until the Father opened the heavens in the Jordan.

What is God's intention in trying us after salvation? Why do we have to go through deserts before going in to the fullness of His purpose?

God's Intention

Let's go back to Israel's experience. The Egyptian army chased them to the shores of the Red Sea. If they went back, they'd surely die. If they went forward to the waters, they had no boats to cross. The two million Israelites were in an impossible situation. They could not go back!

God's intention was to reveal Himself as their all. He just opened the sea and all Israel went across dry land. When the Egyptians wanted to cross the sea, God closed the waters, and they all drowned.

Now at the other side of the sea, the people breathed a sigh of relief. But, did the trials end? They'd just begun.

God brought them to the point of death to teach them trust.

The Crossing

Difficulties were part of Israel's lesson in trusting God:

> *"Thus Israel saw the great work which the LORD had done in Egypt; so the people feared the Lord, and believed the Lord and His servant Moses."*
>
> Exodus 14:31

After the celebration, on the other side of the sea, after seeing God's might deliver them from sure death, Moses ordered the departure towards Shur. But this was harsh, for they found no water (Exodus 15:22).

Have you ever had a day without water? Could you stand to see your children crying for water? The Israelites went through that situation for three days. Many criticize the Jews for the way they behaved in the desert, but the truth is that to go three days without water is very hard. In fact, it is life-threatening. God brought them to the point of death to teach them trust. Though they'd seen the powerful hand of God destroy the Egyptians, the lack of water made them grumble.

The Bitter Water

Following the manifestation of the glory of God before the Israelites in the Red Sea, God takes them to a desert without water. When they reach a place with water— Marah —the spring is bitter (Exodus 14:23).

Why does God allow them to go through three days without water to then take them to bitter waters? I am sure that many people have asked the same question.

In the last years, I have spoken with many believers who have had experiences with God and have no doubt that Jesus saved them. Just as with Israel, their experience of salvation and deliverance was extraordinary, but soon after that the difficulties and bitter experiences began. It is very common to meet believers who, after making a decision to deepen their walk with God, find trials instead of blessings.

It is possible that this is your situation today and that you are not finding solutions to the conflicts. If you are normal, you've tried to figure out why you are in this desert. The people of Israel also reacted, but with muttering.

The Healing of the Waters

Immediately, there is a natural question that arises in those who don't know God:

> *"Now it came to pass, in the morning watch, that the Lord looked down upon the army of the Egyptians through the pillar of fire and cloud, and He troubled the army of the Egyptians."*
>
> Exodus 14:24

The Israelites were worried for their lives and their children's, and they did not understand that God did not want to destroy them. On the contrary, He was close to revealing His purpose to them.

In the same way, God wants to reveal His purpose in the desert, difficulty, or point of death you are facing today. So don't mutter.

> *"And He took off their chariot wheels, so that they drove them with difficulty; and the Egyptians said, "Let us flee from the face of Israel, for the Lord fights for them against the Egyptians."*
>
> Exodus 14:25

God took His people to the bitter water to show them a tree of healing. He is not a destroyer of His children. On the contrary, He has special purposes for them. God wanted to reveal Himself to Israel as its Healer in the place of death(v. 26).

When they arrived at the bitter waters, God brought the Israelites towards the tree of healing that sweetens the bitter waters. He wanted to be a God that sweetens the bitterness.

───────────◆───────────

He wanted to be a God
that sweetens the bitterness.

Here the tree is a symbol of the cross of Christ; the healing of the bitterness of life is found on the cross at Calvary. The only way that God reveals the power of the cross is in the midst of the desert—in other words, in the midst of bitterness.

If you are still looking for the purpose of God in your desert, think of what He showed Israel: The healing was in a tree. In this case God used a tree to manifest a truth: healing on the cross.

God the Healer

In the life of Jesus we see a very powerful truth in regard to His wounds. The Bible states:

> *"But He was wounded for our transgressions, He was bruised for our iniquities; the chastisement of our peace was upon Him, and by His stripes we are healed."*
>
> Isaiah 53:5

A Roman soldier's slashes destroyed the back of our Lord Jesus Christ, but in His wounds we have received healing and salvation. Jesus received authority to heal in the same place that He received His wounds. Our wounds can be transformed into authority to heal and restore.

God wanted to bring Israel to a place of bitterness to show them the healing of the tree. He wanted to heal them to give them more authority. He is Jehovah Raphah, God the Healer.

In the Old Testament, God established that the high priest could not go into His presence with wounds on his body; nor could he offer sacrifices on the altar if he had scabs (Lev. 21:20). A scab is the coagulated blood that stays over the wound when it has begun to heal. The scab shows that the wound has not finished healing yet, and that there is still sensitivity to pain.

God wants to heal all of his children from disease and "scabs." That's why He guides us to bitter places. There He will reveal the name of "Jehovah" and the "Healer." In the place of healing, God will transform our bruises in healing and authority. God wants to reveal Himself as the all in all and the source of all blessing. He wants to heal your bruises and transform them into authority to heal others.

God also wanted to give the Israelites more authority and anointing through this experience; that's why He tested them in Mara. Before giving authority, the Lord tests. If Israel had trusted in God, they would have gone to another spiritual level under open heavens.

Before a promotion or graduation to another spiritual level, God wants to heal us from bruises that we bring from the past. Israel had spent four hundred years in bondage. In all that time they got used to Egypt, doubting their God and trusting in their own strength. In this bitter experience, God wanted to heal them from bitterness.

There is no doubt, in Israel's case the experience was bitter, but God revealed His power. In Jesus' case, it was no easier. He suffered temptation before beginning His ministry of power.

Temptation of Human Nature

After the experience in the Jordan, the Spirit took Jesus to the desert. If at that moment the heavens had been opened, He would have had no need for a desert trial.

Nevertheless, the father wanted to reveal Himself to the Son in new ways.

Jesus had to grow in authority, and that's why the Spirit took Him to the desert. While there He was tempted in the three basic aspects of our human nature:

1. *The Physical Aspect.* The devil told Jesus:

    "If you are the Son of God, command this stone to become bread."

    Luke 4:3

    Jesus had to be tempted in the area of human appetites. He was fasting and it had been forty days since He last ate. God allowed the devil to tempt Him by presenting a way to satisfy His physical hunger. But Jesus answered with the Scripture:

    "It is written, 'Man shall not live by bread alone, but by every word of God."

    Luke 4:4

How could Jesus be the Bread of Life if He did not pass this test? Instead of hunger and thirst, He received from the Father authority to multiply bread and, without selfishness, give it to the needy. He also received authority to deny His desires and put the Father's will in first place.

If you analyze the characteristics of your desert, the temptations that you are suffering, you'll see that God will give you authority in the areas in which He is testing you, but before you receive authority, you must identify your appetites. The devil knows your appetites. He will show them to you, and he will always come to exploit them.

Today I understand that He must test me in those aspects to give me authority, firmness, character, and control over selfish appetites.

In all my years of ministry, I've asked myself why God allows me to go through economic trials, pain, insults, and confrontation with people who question my ministry and character. Today I understand that He must test me in those aspects to give me authority, firmness, character, and control over selfish appetites. It is in difficult places that we will see our appetites and conquer.

Jesus did not respond with an experience. God the Father had just declared that Jesus was the well-pleasing Son, but Jesus did not rely on that experience, He quoted the Word of God. Jesus was going to live by what God the Father said, not by satisfying His appetites.

Why do you want to see God work mightily in your life? Do you know the motives of your heart? Are they to the glory of God or do you just want to be seen as an instrument of God, admired and respected by all? God will expose your appetites until the only hunger you will have is for His voice, His "rhema," His revealed Word.

2. *The Psychological Aspect.* Satan took Jesus to Jerusalem, set Him on the pinnacle of the temple and told Him:

> *"If You are the Son of God, throw Yourself down from here. For it is written, 'He shall give His angels charge over you, to keep you,' and 'In their hands they shall bear you up, lest you dash your foot against a stone.'"*
>
> Luke 4:9–10

The pinnacle was a high place on the temple in Jerusalem. Jesus was tempted to jump, expecting God to send angels to save Him from dying. Even worse, the devil quoted the Word (Psalm 91:11–12). After all, Jesus had declared that He lived by the Word of God, the Rhema Revealed, Timely Word. Therefore, Satan tested Him by quoting Psalm 91. Satan quoted the logos Word. This was a psychological temptation. Satan challenged Jesus to believe in a biblical promise. If He jumped, God should have saved Him.

And Jesus answered and said to him,

> *"It has been said, 'You shall not tempt the Lord your God.'"*
>
> Luke 4:12

When we make a decision thinking that God will back us up because we found a verse in the Bible, we may be tempting God. We challenge God when we make a decision without consent or outside His timing. The only way that Jesus would have jumped was if the Father had told Him to do so. Even if there were a biblical promise, He only obeyed the Father's voice.

How many times have I wanted to copy the decisions of friends in the ministry that led to success. Many Christians expect God to do in them as He does in others. That's not how the things of God work since He has specific plans for each of us.

God's voice in your life
will be your victory.

Some days after the temptation, Jesus had a peculiar experience. After preaching in the synagogue in Nazareth, the Jews got upset and drove Him to the edge of the mountain on which the city was set. They took Him there to throw Him off,

"Then passing through the midst of them, He went His way."
Luke 4:30

Personally, I think the angels transported Jesus and saved Him from death. This was the time to trust God for the protection promised in Psalm 91. Nevertheless, when the devil tempted Him, it was not time to believe but to be tested. Jesus received authority to do the works of the Father since He learned to discern the desires and time of God.

3. *The Spiritual Aspect.*

"Then the devil, taking Him up on a high mountain, showed Him all the kingdoms of the world in a moment of time. And the devil said to Him, 'All this authority I will give You, and their glory; for this has been delivered to me, and I give it to whomever I wish. Therefore, if You will worship before me, all will be Yours."

Luke 4:5–7

Jesus was tempted in the central aspect of His spiritual life. The center of spiritual life is whom you worship. The devil presented Jesus with all the kingdoms of the earth, which He could have taken and reclaimed for God, leaving Satan with nothing.

Nevertheless, Jesus answered:

"Get behind me, Satan! For it is written, 'You shall worship the Lord your God, and Him only you shall serve."

Luke 4:8

Satan wanted to interest Jesus in kingdoms and achieving something great for God, but Jesus was not interested in goals and conquests. He was a worshiper, and the center of His life was His Father.

How many times we're tempted by the devil, who comes along promising things that would appear to be victories for the kingdom of God! But to gain those victories there is a high price to pay as we lose friends, time, physical strength, money, etc.

God is not interested in us conquering great things for Him, but rather that we live in worship and service to Him. For obedience to the Father, Jesus received authority to offer His life as a sacrifice.

In conclusion, the secret of Jesus' victory in the desert was that He heard the voice of the Father and answered with the words of the Father. The only weapon that He used in the desert was "it is written."

The Father opened the heavens in the Jordan and spoke, but this was not the only occasion on which He did so. He continued speaking with His Son until His last breath on the cross. The Holy Spirit took up residence in Jesus and the Father revealed His will. That's why He won and walked His years of ministry under open heavens.

That is precisely what God wanted for Israel and what He wants for us, but we must be willing to hear the voice of the Father.

God Spoke to Israel and Wants to Speak to You

God's desire for the Israelites in the desert is condensed in Exodus 15:26:

> *"And said, 'If you diligently heed the voice of the Lord your God and do what is right in His sight, give ear to His commandments and keep all His statutes, I will put none of the*

diseases on you which I have brought on the Egyptians. For I am the Lord who heals you.'"

The will of God in the desert was that Israel learn to hear and obey His voice. God took them to the desert to speak to them!

◆

God took them to the desert to speak to them!

In your case, God will guide you to a desert because He wants to speak to you, heal you, give you authority, and communicate with you. Nevertheless, God's intention is not only to talk to you in the desert. He wants to make a habitation in your life to talk to you constantly. God's voice in your life will be your victory.

The purpose of the deserts that we go through is that God would speak to us and establish a permanent residence in our lives.

God took Israel to the desert to give them instructions on how to build the tabernacle. This was not a religious building or the symbol of the Jewish religion, but rather a meeting place for God and His people. He wanted to live in the midst of His people.

Purpose of God for Israel

Religious formulas do not bring true worship.

"Thus says the Lord of hosts, the God of Israel: 'Add your burnt offerings to your sacrifices and eat meat. For I did not speak to your fathers, or command them in the day that I

brought them out of the land of Egypt, concerning burnt offerings or sacrifices. But this is what I commanded them, saying, "Obey My voice, and I will be your God, and you shall be My people. And walk in all the ways that I have commanded you, that it may be well with you."'

Jeremiah 7:21–23

The Israelites' greatest worries were the rituals and offerings to God. I never cease to be amazed at how meticulous the Jews are in their service to God. They worry over every last detail of how the Word is read, how to dress, how to pray, what to touch, etc.

Religious people—Christians as well as Jews—worry about these things for they think that they please God, and He is pleased in their obedience. That was God's complaint against Israel.

After many years of history, God tells His people through the prophet Jeremiah that He did not want the excessive sacrifice of animals, nor was that the purpose that He had for them. God's intention was that they learn to heed His voice for them to obey. God didn't take them out of Egypt to be the Jewish religious or the people of sacrifices. He took them out for them to be His family and His habitation on earth.

God's Children

After Satan's defeat in the desert, he did not tempt Him in those areas again. The Father gave Jesus total authority over Satan. After the desert, Jesus was sent to do the works of the Father, and He did what the Father ordained. The Holy Spirit made a permanent habitation in Jesus, who began His ministry as the Son of God. God's sons are those who do the will of the Father. In other words, those who hear His voice and allow Him to set up a permanent habitation in them:

> *"For as many as are led by the Spirit of God, these are sons of God. For you did not receive the spirit of bondage again to fear, but you received the Spirit of adoption by whom we cry out, 'Abba, Father.'"*
>
> Romans 8:14–15

Paul calls this anointing "the spirit of adoption" in order to illustrate the new believer's relationship to the Father.

Paul calls this anointing "the spirit of adoption" in order to illustrate the new believer's relationship to the Father. That new relationship allows us to experience open heavens.

The Power of One

It is a wonderful thing to live as a Christian under open heavens, in perfect obedience and clear communication with the Father. When whole communities of believers begin to live this way, regions begin to be affected and the kingdom of God begins to be truly established.

Now consider the reverse process and you can begin to see the dire importance of some of the decisions Christians make that they mistakenly believe are insignificant.

How are the heavens closed over an area? Sin by sin, person by person, family by family, neighborhood by neighborhood, city by city.

"For sin shall not have dominion over you, for you are not under law but under grace."

Romans 6:14

But we can give sin dominion over our lives and ultimately over our towns and cities. When people begin to disobey habitually in a particular way, they are affecting not only themselves but their entire community. Strongholds result.

---◆---

When people begin to disobey habitually in a particular way, they are affecting not only themselves but their entire community.

Two or three families can cause a ripple effect in a city as they give over contol to habitual gambling, adultery, rebellion, even murder. It's not just that private, personal communion with God is affected. The heavens remain closed over that area.

Some of us who have been tracking the move of God have begun to notice that founders of particular cities have established dominating sins that have, over time, affected generations of inhabitants.

One example is New York City, where the Dutch cheated the original inabitants out of land. The Native Americans then cursed the land with a spirit of violence. Manhattan, the center of the city, has been through decades of violence, marked by stabbings and shootings in the poorer areas, and ruthlessness among the wealthy.

Thankfully, we have seen the violence exposed and pushed back a little in recent years as prayer movements have arisen in the city.

The good news is that when individuals begin to obey God there is also a ripple effect that brings us toward open heavens.

Today's Deserts

The trial of the desert precedes open heavens, because it is in the desert that the Christian learns to hear the voice of God.

To conclude this chapter, I'd like to talk about a desert that many Christians experience when they have to submit to harsh and difficult authorities. It is possible that you are a woman that has to submit to a nonbelieving husband, a husband who needs biblical teaching regarding family. Perhaps you are someone with a call from God who must submit to authorities who do not understand you.

We suffer many trials to which we must submit though we don't like to. Nevertheless, God is preparing us to give us authority and to see open heavens. He declares that, as Jesus submitted we must submit to one another, wives to husbands, husbands to Christ, children to parents, and employees to bosses.

God will reward with authority those who submit.

> *"Wives, likewise, be submissive to your own husbands, that even if some do not obey the word, they, without a word, may be won by the conduct of their wives."*
>
> 1 Peter 3:1

God promises to open the heavens over submissive wives, in such way that their husbands will come without a word. He wants to raise women evangelists, and that's why He prepares them to win people without words.

In the same way, God promises to open the heavens over the husbands, answering their prayers without hindrance.

> *"Husbands, likewise, dwell with them with understanding, giving honor to the wife, as to the weaker vessel, and as being heirs together of the grace of life, that your prayers may not be hindered."*
>
> 1 Peter 3:7

The command is that husbands honor their wives, giving them the same value that God gives them as co-inheritors of His grace.

◆

God wants to raise thousands of men who can be witnesses of His love.

God wants to raise thousands of men who can be witnesses of His love. For this He prepares deserts in which we may show respect to others, starting with our wives.

If you are under an authority that does not understand your spiritual call, don't disobey. Remember that Jesus waited for the day of His manifestation. If you wait, the Father will manifest His pleasure over your life, and He'll rejoice in your ministry.

After the bitter experience of Israel, God revealed His power. After the forty days of temptation of Christ,

He began His ministry of power. After all trials we will be filled with the Spirit, according to the Father's promise.

9

The Purpose of the Promise of the Holy Spirit

In the experience of the Jordan, Jesus received the fullness of the Holy Spirit. From that moment on, the Spirit anointed Him to fulfill the purpose for which His Father had called Him:

> *"The Spirit of the Lord is upon me, because He has anointed Me to preach the gospel to the poor; He has sent me to heal the brokenhearted, to proclaim liberty to the captives, and recovering of sight to the blind, to set at liberty those who are oppressed, to proclaim the acceptable year of the Lord."*
>
> Luke 4:18–19

The anointing of the Holy Spirit is not an isolated experience or a simple blessing; it is useful in fulfilling the divine purposes.

The Father sent His Son, Jesus, with the purpose of announcing the good news of salvation, deliverance, and grace, and to destroy the curse of sin that separates us from His good desires.

The Father's desire is to have a paternal, loving and

caring relationship with His children, but Adam's disobedience (his sin) obstructs the fulfillment of this desire. So God sent Jesus with the purpose of restoring the relationship with His children, that He may be the all in all.

To fulfill the desire of His Father, Jesus not only needed to be filled with the anointing of the Holy Spirit, but also filled with the glory of the Father to carry out God's work.

Jesus had to hear and obey the Father's voice constantly, and the death on the cross was the last step of obedience.

Earlier I spoke of how Jesus, being like the Father, left it all to live as a servant. That process of leaving did not allow Him to know the will of the Father on His own.

Jesus had to hear and obey the Father's voice constantly, and the death on the cross was the last step of obedience. The Father's desires could not be met without the remission of our sins, which had to be paid with the shedding of the blood of the Lamb of God. That is why Jesus submitted to the Father, since He never acted on His own will. On the contrary, since He was one with the Father, He did only what He showed Him to do.

Jesus Does What the Father Does

Why did Jesus do what the Father showed Him to do? The Lord himself explained:

> *"Then Jesus answered and said to them, 'Most assuredly, I say to you, the Son can do nothing of Himself, but whatever*

He sees the Father do; for whatever He does, the Son also does in like manner. For the Father loves the Son, and shows Him all things that He Himself does; and He will show Him greater works than these, that you may marvel. . . . I can of Myself do nothing. As I hear, I judge; and My judgment is righteous, because I do not seek My own will but the will of the Father who sent Me."

John 5:19–20, 30

Ever since His baptism, Jesus had to see what the Father did, and that's why He needed open heavens. He had to be the visible manifestation of the Father that announced the good news, healed sick, set captives free, raised the dead, and forgave sin.

When the disciples wanted to see the Father, Jesus answered that, by seeing Him, they were seeing the Father. Jesus was the only man filled with the Father's glory. That's why the Father was pleased.

The Father's Example

As parents we rejoice as we see our children grow, but, above all, we feel pleased when, due to good preparation in the home and our example, our children follow our steps and emulate our behavior. How great it is as parents when our children tell us that they want to be like us.

Jesus pleased the Father when He submitted to John's baptism and let the Spirit fill Him with the glory of God. The Spirit not only anointed Him with power and authority, but also gave Him the Father's heart, allowing Him to feel what God felt.

The Father needed to show Jesus all that was done

in the heavens. Therefore Jesus needed open heavens, perfect communication with no hindrance. He needed to hear the Father's voice to evaluate all experiences on earth.

Jesus had to satisfy the will and the desires of the Father. That's why He needed open heavens to know the Father's heart.

The Father's Promise to the Church

When Jesus described "the Father's promise" as the baptism in the Holy Spirit or filling with power from above, He was not talking about salvation, but something different.

Before His death, Jesus was saying goodbye to His disciples (John 12). He announced Judas' betrayal (John 13). Then He consoled them with these words:

> *"Let not your heart be troubled: you believe in God, believe also in Me. In my Father's house are many mansions: if it were not so, I would have told you. I go to prepare a place for you. And if I go and prepare a place for you, I will come again, and receive you to Myself; that where I am, there you may be also."*
>
> John 14:1–3

Jesus was very clear with His disciples. He told them that He was going to leave them, that He was going to die, and that He had to go prepare place for them in His Father's house. They were worried, but He gave them a promise:

"If you love Me, keep my commandments. And I will pray the Father, and He will you another Helper that He may abide with you for ever—the Spirit of truth; whom the world cannot receive, because it neither sees Him nor knows Him; but you know Him; for he dwells with you, and will be in you. I will not leave you orphans; I will come to you. Yet a little while, and the world will see Me no more; but you will see Me. Because I live, you will live also. At that day you will know that I am in My Father, and you in Me, and I in you."

John 14:15–20

═══════════◆═══════════
Jesus consoled His disciples
with a promise.
═══════════════════════

Jesus consoled His disciples with a promise. Though the world would not see Him any more, they would see Him. Though, according to human logic, He was going to disappear from this earth, they would see Him again. The Holy Spirit would be sent that Jesus might be seen. But there is more.

Three Revelations

On the day that the Holy Spirit would be sent, the disciples knew that Jesus was in the Father, they were in Jesus, and Jesus in them.

The coming of the Spirit would produce three revelations in the life of the church:

First: Jesus is in the Father. The preposition *in* refers to Jesus' place, time, and state. His position in the place is at the right hand of the Father, His time position is eternal, and His state of being is King of Kings and Lord of Lords.

The position of Jesus glorified and exalted is the reward of the obedience and sacrifice of the Son of God, the fulfillment of His work on earth and His victory.

━━━━━━━━━━━ ◆ ━━━━━━━━━━━

The coming of the Holy Spirit was, for the disciples, the proof that Jesus had arrived in heaven and had occupied His place.

The coming of the Holy Spirit was, for the disciples, the proof that Jesus had arrived in heaven and had occupied His place.

Second: The church is in Jesus. The preposition *in* here refers to the position of the church in Christ. To be in Christ means to be one with Him. The arrival of the Father's promise was proof that Jesus was with the Father. Thus, the church had the same position.

We are one with Jesus: (1) in His exaltation and victory against Satan, therefore His victory is also ours; (2) in sharing His throne, sitting in high places with access to the Father; (3) in our relationship with the Father. God accepts us in Him and loves us with the same love that He loves the Son.

Third: Jesus is in the church. The life, glory, and presence of Jesus are not only manifested in heaven, but also in the church, in other words in our lives.

Jesus is in the church through the Holy Spirit who came to: (1) confirm the final victory of Jesus in His exaltation and glory in our lives; (2) manifest the presence of the glorified Jesus in the hearts of the first members of the church; (3) share the victory and the glory of Christ in the church; (4) share the joy and the power of Christ sitting in the throne of glory.

These revelations are possible thanks to the promise of the Father, the same one that Jesus made to His disciples.

The Waiting

Though Jesus walked with open heavens through the Holy Spirit, He could not baptize anyone. In the power of the baptism of the Spirit He had to, first of all, confront temptation and defeat it. Second, He had to live the next three years in the power of the Spirit, manifesting the glory of the Father. And, third, He had to offer Himself to God as a sacrifice.

The Father wanted to restore the relationship with His sons, but Jesus had to live a perfect life and die on the cross. Only after the final obedience of Jesus, would the Father give the Son the authority to give others the same power, that is the anointing of open heavens.

Jesus taught the disciples "by the Holy Spirit for forty days" (Acts 1:2,3), and before returning to heaven, He reminded them of the promise of the Father:

"And, being assembled together with them, He commanded them not to depart from Jerusalem, but to wait for the Promise of the Father, 'which,' He said,'you have heard from me. For John truly baptized with water; but you shall be baptized with the Holy Spirit not many days from now'" (Acts 1:4–5).

"Behold, I send the promise of My Father upon you: but tarry in the city of Jerusalem, until you are endued with power from on high" (Luke 24:49).

Ever since that moment, the disciples had to continue Jesus' mission on earth. Nevertheless, alone they could do nothing. They had to wait for the anointing of the Holy Spirit.

The Filling of Jesus and the Church

The disciples needed to see open heavens over their lives and receive the promise of the Father—the Holy Spirit. The same one that Jesus received in the Jordan was also for the church, and Jesus would baptize it with the Spirit.

The disciples needed to see open heavens over their lives and receive the promise of the Father—the Holy Spirit.

"Upon whom you shall see the Spirit descending, and remaining on Him, this is He who baptizes with the Holy Spirit."
John 1:33

The church will need to fulfill the task of being a witness of Jesus on earth. For this it needs the power of the Holy Spirit. In other words, open heavens.

Jesus received the filling on behalf of the whole church. That is all it needs in order to walk with open heavens. Once Jesus received the promise of the Father, He was ready to impart it. He is the one who baptizes and the one who opens the heavens.

The apostle Peter, in regard to Jesus, states:

"Therefore being exalted to the right hand of God, and having received from the Father the Promise of the Holy Spirit, he poured out this which you now see and hear."
Acts 2:33

When Jesus ascended to heaven, God made Him "Lord and Christ" (Acts 2:36) and received the promise of the Father—the baptism of the Holy Spirit. In the Jordan He had received the filling of the Spirit to carry out the Father's will. In heaven, He received the filling of the Spirit for us to do His will on earth, for us to enjoy open heavens.

Advantages of Open Heavens

When the heavens opened over the church, Jesus' promise to the disciples came true:

> *"And He said to him, 'Most assuredly, I say to you, hereafter you shall see heaven open, and the angels of God ascending and descending upon the Son of man.'"*
>
> John 1:51

Jesus said that the manifestation of open heavens would be seen over the Son of Man. Open heavens have to do with the manifestation of the glorified Christ. Even angelic manifestations are based on the person of Jesus and the victory of the Son of God.

Let's take stock of the many benefits and blessings that come with open heavens:

- The angels, as a heavenly army, manifest the power, glory, and triumph of the victorious Jesus.
- The glory of Christ is made manifest, not on heaven's throne, but ascending and descending from earth to heaven and heaven to earth.
- Our worship, praise, prayer, and intercession are

based in the victory of the glorified Christ and rise as an acceptable sacrifice.

- Our worship rises, not on a ladder, but rather on the presence of Christ in the midst of us.
- Our worship goes to the throne of God as a victorious cry of a church that is more than a conqueror.
- Prayer goes to the throne of grace and fills it with incense pleasing to the Father.
- Our worship and praise is lifted not by means of human techniques, nor intellectual or emotional efforts, but by the simple faith of a sincere heart, sure that Jesus' victory is total, unquestionable, absolute, and real.

The life and the activities of heaven
are manifested on earth.

- Our service, which is the genuine exaltation of the glorified Christ, comes to the throne of the Father. When our service arrives the Father is pleased, and He manifests His delight.
- The life of the glorified and exalted Jesus descends. The victory of Christ over death, sin, the world, and Satan is not limited to heaven. It descends from heaven to earth and our lives.
- The power of life that defeats the power of death descends to manifest against any power, influence, idea, or demon in our lives.
- The glory of Jesus' victory is manifested in our lives as a testimony to the world.
- The victory of the glorified Christ descends from heaven to manifest in our lives against all tempta-

tions, all satanic plans of destruction, and anything that hinders the knowledge of God.
• The life and the activities of heaven are manifested on earth.

When the heavens open, the church is able to communicate the message of reconciliation.

Reconciliation with God

Jesus came to do the works of the Father, and that's why He was filled with the glory of God through the Spirit. The Christian comes to do the works of Jesus thus, he must be filled with the glory of the glorified Christ, through the Holy Spirit. This happened on the day of Pentecost when the heavens opened over the church. Jesus carried out the will of the Father as He reconciled man with Him. The Christian carries out the will of the Son:

> *"Now all things are of God, who has reconciled us to himself through Jesus Christ, and has given us the ministry of reconciliation; that is, that God was in Christ, reconciling the world to Himself, not imputing their trespasses to them; and has committed to us the word of reconciliation. Now then, we are ambassadors for Christ, as though God were pleading through us: we implore you on Christ's behalf, be reconciled to God."*
>
> 2 Cor. 5:18–20

The Father reconciled the world to Himself through the sacrifice of the Son. Jesus reconciled the world with the Father by obeying the Father unto death. The Christian reconciles the world with God by being an ambassador in the name of Jesus.

◆

Jesus reconciled the world with the
Father by obeying the Father unto death.

Jesus as a Priority

You may be asking yourself: How can I be an ambassador in the name of Jesus and experience open heavens in my life? Jesus has a simple answer:

> *"On the last day, that great day of the feast, Jesus stood and cried out, saying, 'If anyone thirsts, let him come to Me, and drink. He who believes in me, as the Scripture has said, out of his heart shall flow rivers of living water.' But this He spoke concerning the Spirit, whom those believing in Him would receive; for the Holy Spirit was not yet given; because Jesus was not yet glorified."*
>
> John 7:37–39

The first requirement for being an ambassador is to be hungry for the life of the glorified Christ who is sitting at the right hand of the Father and has all authority in heaven and earth. The second requirement is to drink of Christ. We drink of Him when we believe without doubt in Him and His promises, and we set our sight only on Him. To believe in Him is to develop a life of communion with Him as a priority, surrender to His Word, and trust in His faithfulness.

Have you settled for forgiveness in the cross? Believe in Him that baptizes in the Holy Spirit. Believe that the glory manifests with the power of the Holy Spirit. Rivers of living water, open heavens, are manifested in those who surrender to the Holy Spirit and wait on Him. The rivers of living water represent the life of the resurrected and exalted Christ who reigns as Lord and King.

Christ Glorified in Your Life

In chapter six, I spoke of the veil that may be covering our hearts, which prevents the life of Christ from being seen by a dying world. The glorified Christ has saved us and lives in our hearts to manifest His power and victory, but there is a veil that covers it, as happened in the temple of Jerusalem and the tabernacle of Moses. The glory of God was manifest in the holy place, but there was a veil that did not allow it to be seen.

We said that the veil of our flesh, of our humanity and our doubts was removed and broken when we turned toward the Spirit. When we are thirsty for that revelation and we believe that it is for us, the Holy Spirit glorifies Jesus in our souls.

At that moment you begin to:

- Set your eyes on the complete work of Jesus over every manifestation of the flesh
- Believe that Jesus has absolute power over anything that opposes your growth
- See the closeness of the presence of God
- Rest in the protection of Christ victorious
- Dwell in the holy place or place of intimacy

It will be then that you will see open heavens mani-fested on earth. This manifestation will be as a river of living water flowing and imparting life to all who submerge in it.

━━━━━━━━━━ ✦ ━━━━━━━━━━

This manifestation will be as a river of living water flowing and imparting life to all who submerge in it.

In Essence

The Holy Spirit is essential to the church. In this chapter we saw that:

1. To fulfill God's purposes, the anointing of the Spirit is necessary.
2. The promise of the Father is the promise of the Holy Spirit.
3. With the Spirit, we are one with the Father and the Son.
4. With the Holy Spirit, we have the advantages of the open heavens.

Though we believe in the promise of the Father, we have not been experiencing it to the fullest. These are the days in which we will see this promise fulfilled. God is anointing His army.

10

God Anoints His Army

In the book of Acts we find the model of a church that walked continually under open heavens. This is what God wants to see throughout the nations. Recounted here are the events in Ephesus when the heavens were opened over the city.

Let's see the progress of this passage:

1. Paul came to Ephesus and encountered a group of some twelve disciples and asked them:

    "Did you receive the Holy Spirit when you believed?"
    Acts19:2

    The baptism that these people received was of John, in other words, the baptism of repentance.
2. John had baptized many Jews and had told them to believe in Jesus, the Christ (Acts 19:4). As Paul had the task of conquering the city of Ephesus, he laid his hands on these believers and prayed that they would be filled with the Holy Spirit.

    In the same way that Jesus was filled in the Jordan, these men received the fullness of the power and anointing of the Spirit and spoke in other tongues and prophesied (Acts 19:6).

3. After the Holy Spirit filled these Ephesian disciples, Paul preached the message of the kingdom and announced the coming of it to the nations.

"And he went into the synagogue, and spoke boldly for three months, reasoning and persuading concerning the things of the kingdom of God."

Acts 19:8

The Holy Spirit now presses the army to invade the cities announcing that Jesus is King and that He wants to reign over every life.

4. Along with the message of the kingdom being announced, the name of Jesus was glorified with wonders

"Now God worked unusual miracles by the hands of Paul, so that even handkerchiefs or aprons were brought from his body to the sick and the diseases left them and the evil spirits went out of them."

Acts 19:11–12

When the heavens are open over the city, God begins to back up the preaching of the gospel with healing and miracles. Jesus promised that signs would follow those who believe (Mark 16:17). The purpose of the signs in the conquering of a city is simply to show evidence of the Lordship of Jesus over illnesses that are a product of sin.

5. Under open heavens, the spiritual world is dominated. The church defeats the evil spirits of the city. When this happens, the commotion of the demonic world is the best advertising for the gospel.

"Then some of the itinerant Jewish exorcists took it upon themselves to call the name of the Lord Jesus over those who had evil spirits, saying, 'We exorcise you by the Jesus whom Paul preaches.' Also there were seven sons of Sceva, a Jewish chief priest, who did so. And the evil spirit answered and said, 'Jesus I know, and Paul I know; but who are you?' Then the man in whom the evil spirit was leaped on them, overpowered them, and prevailed against them, so that they fled out of that house naked and wounded. This became known both to all Jews and Greeks dwelling in Ephesus; and fear fell on them all, and the name of the Lord Jesus was magnified."

Acts 19:13–17

The evil spirit that was in the Ephesian man, declared that he "knew Jesus." If we paraphrase this expression it would have said something like this: "I have experience with Jesus, and I know what the consequences are of an encounter with Him." When the demon declared this truth, it was known in the whole city, and the name of Jesus was magnified. Under open heavens, even the demons preach on the power of Jesus.

━━━━━━━━━ ◆ ━━━━━━━━━
Under open heavens, even the demons admit the lordship of Jesus.
━━━━━━━━━━━━━━━━━━━

6. When the heavens are open over a city, the demons are bound. Repentance is manifested in the church:

"many of the ones that had believed saw, confessed, and gave an account of their acts."

Acts 19:18

I think that the attitudes of pride, and the religious appearances are the product of satanic work within the church, but when the Lord is magnified, Christians are the first to confess hidden sins and secret heart attitudes.

7. Anointed preaching of the gospel of the kingdom, the miracles, and the dominion over the demonic world in Ephesus caused great disturbance:

"And the same time there arose a great commotion about the Way."

Acts 19:23

The city of Ephesus was the heart of the cult of the goddess Diana. The temple and entire religious structure dedicated to this particular idol were headquartered here. Open heavens over Ephesus diminished the popularity of the Diana cult.

In response, Demetrius, a metal worker who made small statues of Diana organized a protest due to the influence of the Christians. The craftsmen lost a lot of money because the people would not buy their products. The principality over this city—named Diana—was defeated.

---◆---

When the heavens are open over a city, it is not even necessary to mention the principalities by name.

The city was filled with confusion, and all of Diana's followers went to the theatre to protest.

There they asked for the destruction of the church and the death of Paul. Nevertheless,

"since these things cannot be denied, you ought to be quiet and do nothing rashly. For you have brought these men here who are neither robbers of temples nor blasphemers of your goddess."

Acts 19:36–37

When the heavens are open over a city, it is not even necessary to mention the principalities by name. Paul and the church did not need to give seminars regarding the tactics and beliefs of Diana's cult. They did not even have to mention it by name. God opened the heavens and the cult of Diana was defeated.

There is no doubt when the heavens are open that the enemy is defeated. But if we want to live continuously under open heavens, we must keep the fire of our first love burning. Look what happened to the church at Ephesus.

First Works

The church in Ephesus is the model of the church that walked with open heavens. Nevertheless thirty years after this experience, Jesus said to this same church:

"I know your works, your labor, and your patience, and that you cannot bear those who are evil. And you have tested those who say they are apostles and are not, and have found them liars; and you have persevered and have patience and have labored for My name's sake and have not become weary.

Nevertheless I have this against you, that you have left your first love. Remember therefore from where you have fallen; repent, and do the first works; or else I will come to you quickly, and remove your lampstand from its place—unless you repent . . . He who has an ear, let him hear what the Spirit says to the churches; To him who overcomes I will give to eat from the tree of life, which is in the midst of the Paradise of God."

Rev 2:2–5,7

This is Jesus' call to the church: Come back to your first love. Do the first works. These are the works that the believers did in Ephesus for the heavens to open:

- Believed and were baptized in the name of Jesus
- Received the fullness of the Holy Spirit
- Preached the message of the gospel
- prayed for the sick and saw wonders
- Took dominion over the demons and cast them out
- Defeated the principality of the region, and declared Jesus as King

It is necessary that the church keep its victories, for the day that the army of God will conquer the world for Christ is at hand.

The Conquest

From the book of Joshua, we know that the Israelites went through the Jordan and entered the Promised Land. Nevertheless, they had a great task before them: the conquest. God has given us great promises, but just like Israel, we must conquer them.

The book of Judges tells about the conquest of Canaan. In chapter 1, God shows His strategy: First, Judah would go up to defeat the people who inhabited the territory. Then the other tribes would "evict" them. God wanted to use the whole people in the process, who did not belong to any leader or tribe in particular. Each one had a role. God had anointed all of Israel to defeat the enemy and throw them out of the land.

God has given us great promises, but just like Israel, we must conquer them.

What happened in the conquest? The Israelites disobeyed God and did not follow the divine strategy. God had ordered Judah to go fight against the Canaanites, but he looked for human help from his brother Simeon (Judges 1:2–3).

When the other tribes went over to the territory of their defeated enemies, they did not cast them but kept them to work the land (Judges 1:21). This disobedience brought great losses to Israel.

As Christians, we must be obedient and surrender to God, for He wants to open the heavens over each of His children.

God Wants to Anoint His People

It's tragic: There is no demon powerful enough to oppress a Christian, but when God gives us over to the hands of our oppressors because of our own disobedience, we suffer painful consequences.

Israel cried, and God raised judges. These were men

and women anointed to defeat the enemy. Glory to God for the men and women who have risen to bring liberty, blessing, and salvation to the people of God!

God raised those judges because Israel disobeyed the original plan. His initial desire was to use everyone in the conquest of the land and the total destruction of the people.

In the beginning of the book of Judges, everyone fought, but at the end the only one really fighting was Samson. What a tragedy!

In recent years in the Church we have seen how God has raised many men and women anointed to bring liberty and healing to the nations. He's had to raise these people to reestablish truths that have been overlooked and were slowly lost in the Church.

They have gifts of healing, ministries of anointing, power, and deliverance, and evangelistic burden and zeal for the Word of God. He raised these instruments because we've forgotten to pray for the sick, take authority over demons, preach the gospel on the street, and study the Word, as we've forgotten to depend on Him. Thank God for these leaders that He has anointed.

He would like to anoint the whole body
for the latter day conquest.

Nevertheless, today God also is anointing His people. He does not want to anoint only the few willing to pay the price and carry the burden for the work of God. He would like to anoint the whole body for the latter day conquest. He wants to open the heaven over all His children.

The Anointing is for All

In the same way that the heavens opened over Jesus to do the work of the Father, also should they open over all Christians to do the work of Christ. Jesus promised that we would do greater works, for He would go to the Father and whatever we'd ask in His name would be done.

As a minister, I know that my responsibility before the Lord is to minister what God gives me. My function has been to receive from God through prayer, and the studying of the Word. In this process, I have received power, anointing, and truth to share with needy people. But today, God is not just anointing choice servants for the works of ministry. God is anointing His people.

For example, in the ministry where I served the Lord for several years, I served alongside a group of more than fifty employees. Though these men and women of God had worked very hard, I was seen as the anointed, the mouthpiece that God used. When the Lord led me to study the book of Judges with all of them, we realized together that God wanted to anoint all of us for the battle.

Today we see that the "stars" are disappearing and that God uses His people in the revivals that are taking place in Pensacola, Toronto, Buenos Aires, and Bogota, to mention a few.

It is the Spirit that Ministers

The first time I visited Toronto Christian Airport Fellowship, I noticed that no one person shined. The pastor was sitting in the first row, dressed like any other person. At the end of the meeting, I approached the altar, to be one of the first to be ministered to when the call was made.

I wanted the preacher to lay hands on me and pray for me. When the moment arrived, the preacher disappeared, and I stood waiting at the altar. All of a sudden, all over the sanctuary, more than two hundred church ministry team members appeared, designated to pray for those who had walked to the front.

Near the group I was in, a young man with long hair, jeans, and a T-shirt was assigned to pray for the people. I thought, "This boy is not going to pray for me, I want it to be a pastor or the preacher." The Holy Spirit rebuked me and told me that He would be the one ministering to me no matter what person He used.

I can't remember who ministered to me, but I received a powerful touch of the Spirit.

I can't remember who ministered to me, but I received a powerful touch of the Spirit. My life was transformed again. The anointing was not deposited in the preacher or some select group. The heavens were over the whole congregation.

The Ministry at the Radio Station.

During the month of October 1997, the Spirit confirmed this truth to my heart. Thousands of people, hungry for a touch from God, came to our station to be prayed for. We had to stop the work to minister to them, and we decided that we'd limit office work to two hours a day so that we could minister to everyone who came.

The New Jerusalem

God's desire is to glorify Himself through all believers and not a select few. That time is over. This is the time of conquest that will be carried out by a people: the church of the Lord Jesus Christ. Though we thank God for the men that He has anointed powerfully, we know that He is raising an army that will manifest His glory to the nations.

God is opening the heavens over a people of conquest:

> *"And the nations of those who are saved shall walk in its light: and the kings of the earth bring their glory and honor into it. Its gates shall not be shut at all by day: (there shall be no night there). And they shall bring the glory and the honor of the nations into it."*
>
> Rev. 21:24–26

In the New Jerusalem, the nations will worship the Lord Almighty and the Lamb, offering Him their glory and honor. Each nation will bring their particular glory and honor, because He has gifted every nation on earth with a spiritual glory and honor. In the same way, He has given each church spiritual weapons so that they might be part of the army of God.

The Army of God

Just as Japan is known worldwide for its electronics, Germany for its precision, Italy for its food, Argentina for its meats, Mexico for its music, and Greece for its philosophy, each nation has received from God a spiritual gifting.

God will raise the Church in each nation to walk and use the spiritual capabilities that it has received. The army of God in the latter days won't use strategies, talent or human abilities, rather it will move in unity from place to place saving souls and destroying the works of the devil. This army will move under open heavens, and the glory of God will guide them.

How Will the Army of God Be?

The prophet Joel warns: "Blow the trumpet in Zion, and sound an alarm in my holy mountain" (Joel 2:1).

―――――◆―――――
God will raise the church in each nation
to go out and conquer using the spiritual
ability it has received.

Before the army of God arises, the spirit of prophecy will declare that the trumpet must be blown in Zion. The horn was blown to call the people together for war.

"A day of darkness and of gloominess, a day of clouds and of thick darkness, like the morning clouds spread over the mountains: a people come, great an strong, the like of whom has never been seen, nor will there ever be any such after them, even for many successive generations."

Joel 2:2

God will raise the church in each nation to go out and conquer using the spiritual ability it has received.

This army will rise in days of darkness, but it will be a great army. God has never commissioned an army like the one for the latter days.

> *"A fire devours before them; and behind them a flame burns: the land is like the Garden of Eden before them, and behind them a desolate wilderness; surely nothing shall escape them."*
>
> Joel 2:3

The expression "consuming fire" is very common in the Bible, and it is used when talking about the fire on Mount Sinai that lit the burning bush before Moses. This was the glory of God manifested as fire. Likewise, this consuming fire is the glory of God in the mouth of this army that will declare the Word of God over the nations. With the Word of fire anything can be consumed, though it be like the Garden of Eden.

> *"Their appearance is like the appearance of horses; and like swift steeds, so they run. With a noise like chariots over mountaintops they leap, like the noise of a flaming fire that devours the stubble, as a strong people set in battle array. Before them, the people writhe in pain. All faces are drained of color."*
>
> Joel 2:4–6

When there is open heaven over the church, the takeover is quick and without obstacles. If there are mountains or walls, the army of God will go over them in a supernatural way. Though the human power opposes, this army will cause its enemies to fear.

201

"They run like mighty men; they climb the wall like men of war; every one marches in formation, and they do not break ranks. They do not push one another; every one marches in his own column, though they lunge between the weapons, they are not cut down."

Joel 2:7–8

With open heavens, the people of God will have a conquest task. Each part of this army will fulfill its purpose: each division and platoon will have its own task that will not compare to the next and there will not be jealousy or division among them. They will all be very busy going over walls of impossibilities and miracles that previously had stopped the conquest. Though the enemy will prepare arms for destruction, this army will not be affected because it will walk under open heavens.

"The earth quakes before them; the heavens tremble: the sun and the moon grow dark, and the stars diminish their brightness."

Joel 2:10

♦

Nature itself will testify of the power of God through the Church.

This will be a supernatural army. Nature itself will testify of the power of God through the Church, and, of course, she will obey the orders of her General.

God's Orders for His Army

A few months ago I was in prayer, and I was meditating on God's call to the church of the last days: possess the nations. I asked myself: How is this going to happen and with what resources? I sensed from the Spirit of the Lord that hearts would not be moved even if we were to gather millions in every major stadium in the world. Nevertheless, the hearts would move to the breaking point if someone—a child, a young person or elder—were to step out and declare that there would be no rain if he or she ordered it. Jonah went to Nineveh and the whole nation repented. His message was very simple and consisted of eight words:

> *"And Jonah began to enter the city on the first day's walk. Then he cried out and said, "Yet forty days, and Nineveh shall be overthrown."*

Jonah 3:4

Jonah declared eight words over Nineveh, and they all repented. That is proof that he was under open heavens.

The army of God will declare wonders in nature, and the nations will come to Jesus' feet.

> *"The Lord gives voice before His army, for His camp is very great; for strong is the One who executes His word. For the ay of the Lord is great and very terrible; Who can endure it?"*

Joel 2:11

This is the army of God, and He is the one to give orders. In Joel 1, God talks about an army of locusts that will bring judgment and destruction to earth. Many of us think that the army in chapter two is the same as in chapter one. Nevertheless, chapter two is an army that

God is raising. He gives the orders that are executed by a numerous and powerful people.

Therefore we must prepare and humble ourselves before the presence of God.

The Spirit's Exhortation to Repentance

Finally, Jesus said:

> *"And this gospel of the kingdom will be preached in all the world as a witness to all the nations; and then the end will come."*
>
> Mathew 24:14

The message of the kingdom is not a message of a poor suffering Savior, but that of a King whose name is Jesus, also known as the Lord of lords and King of kings. His army will preach in all nations under open heavens "as a witness."

His army will preach in all nations under open heavens "as a witness."

A witness is brought in to a judicial proceeding to give evidence. This message will be declared with evidence or proof that will leave no doubt that Jesus is King. That's why the Bible talks about evidence in nature, of soldiers who fall on their swords, and people who will be mortally wounded and will not die. God will show the nations evidence of power through His church. That's why Joel ends with these words:

> *"'Now, therefore,' says the Lord, 'turn to Me with all your heart, with fasting, with weeping and with mourning.' So rend your hearts and not your garments; return to the Lord your God, for He is gracious and merciful, slow to anger and of great kindness; and He relents from doing harm."*
>
> Joel 2:12–13

As I said in chapter six, there is a veil that is covering what Jesus is writing in our hearts. He is writing the gospel of the kingdom in our lives. Nevertheless, for His message to manifest, we must "convert," turn to the Holy Spirit, and depend on Him.

Joel exhorts us and directs us to turn to the Holy Spirit with the weeping and mourning of repentance, rending our hearts. This way we will see the merciful heart of the Lord.

Get ready, do not doubt your destiny in God, for He has started to open the heavens over the Church, and this is the beginning. You will be part of the army that will conquer the nations for the Lord, and you will see open heavens in your home, community, city, and nation.

Are you willing to trust in God? Are you willing to stay under the hand of God until the day of manifestation comes? The Holy Spirit has spoken to the Church these days through prophetic voices that foretell what is coming. Throughout the nation there are groups that are waiting for an awesome revival.

Epilogue

I would like to tell you what I have perceived from the Holy Spirit while writing this book. The promises in Hebrews 12:22–24 will be fulfilled:

> *"You have come to Mount Zion and to the city of the living God, the heavenly Jerusalem, to an innumerable company of angels, to the general assembly and church of the first born who are registered in heaven, to God the judge of all, to the spirits of just men made perfect, to Jesus the mediator of the new covenant, and to the blood of sprinkling that speaks of better things than that of Abel."*

We have come to Mount Zion. Zion is the place where God shines, the place where He has set His throne to rule and reign. We have come near to the days where God will shine. No one else will, except Him. People will come to our gatherings to see God in all of His splendor. He will receive the glory. The glory given to men, institutions, and traditions will fade. God will be seen.

We have come to the city of the Living God. Zion is the place and the experience in which God will not be seen just as truth, a message, or a service. God will be experienced as a living, real, tangible Father. Imagine, we won't have to try to convince anyone to come to

God. They will come because He will manifest His real presence.

We will come to the heavenly Jerusalem, to an innumerable company of angels. Although the heavenly Jerusalem is in the heavens, and one day the whole world will see it suspended over the city of earthly Jerusalem, we have come near that heavenly city, where the throne is, where the river of God is flowing to the healing of the nations. I believe that in some way, for the first time in history, the church of Jesus Christ will be connected spiritually with the heavenly Jerusalem, and the life and power that flows there will flow through us for the healing and restoration of many. We are about to see the "stair" of open heaven come down and angels will ascend and descend from that heavenly city to our cities, with miracles, revelation, mighty manifestations of power, and healing to whole nations.

We are to become the church of the First-Born. God will change our name. We will lose names, traditions, and distinctives. The first-born in Israel received double-portion inheritance. Elisha called Elijah, "My Father." When Elijah died, Elisha claimed the double-portion as the first-born. We are the first-born after Jesus, the Anointed. We will move with a double portion anointing over the earth, and we will do greater works than Jesus.

God will Judge all. We are near the great manifestation of the judgments of God upon the earth. The only difference is that God will manifest His righteous judgement in order to lead men to repentance, not to punish. God, in His mercy will allow judgments in nature, in economies, shaking the nations as the prophets foretold. These judgments will create huge movements of repentance and weeping over whole cities. Expect God to show

Himself through world conflicts, natural disasters, and crisis. Men will turn to Him.

We have come near to the spirits of just men made perfect. We are coming near to the spiritual anointing left here by godly men and women that have gone on to be with the Lord. When Elijah was taken, he left his mantle; he did not take it to heaven. No one needs the anointing in heaven. It is left here for someone else to use. Ask for the anointing that men and women of God have left for us.

The blood that speaks refers to the authority of the blood. The blood not only covers our sin and washes away the guilt of our sins, but it speaks with power. It shouts around us, and it warns the enemy to beware. That revelation will stir boldness in us that will raise an army of unstoppable believers.

God will open the heavens over all nations, and Jesus Christ will be glorified.

Before Jesus returns to claim His Bride, we will see the greatest harvest of souls in the history of mankind. This harvest will not take a long time to be produced. It will come fast and furious. It will consume all of our time. We will be free from the cares of the world. We will see the greater glory, one greater than the glory of the first century church.

"And the earth will be filled with the knowledge of the glory of the Lord as the waters cover the sea."